/10 Leslie

INFERNAL CHILD

L.H love

E. Pizzey.

7/04/05.

Forthcoming

The Sluts and Lovers Cookbook

Infernal Child

World without Love

Erin Pizzey

Little Hermit Press

*To Christopher and to all the mothers,
children and staff who have passed
through Chiswick Women's Aid*

CONTENTS

	Prologue	11
1	China, South Africa, Beirut	20
2	North America	27
3	Teheran	34
4	England: School and St Mary's	45
5	England: Lethal Games	69
6	Dakar	79
7	England Again: Streatham and Bridport	89
8	Macao and Hong Kong	97
9	England: The Last Act	108
	Epilogue	116

Erin Pizzey, born in 1939, returned to England from the Far East in 1960, and founded Chiswick Women's Aid in 1971. Her book, *Scream Quietly or the Neighbours Will Hear*, was published as a Penguin Special in 1974. It was the first book in the world on wife battering.

International author, published poet and playwright, Erin Pizzey is the international founder of refuges for battered women and children. Author of many novels, and non-fiction as well as articles for the *New Statesman*, *The Sunday Times*, *Cosmopolitan* and many other journals, magazines and newspapers worldwide she is well known for her work with the less privileged. Erin Pizzey's name is known throughout Britain and many other parts of the world as that of the courageous and indomitable champion of battered women. Her refusal to say no to women in need has brought her into constant conflict with the authorities, but in her view the simple rightness of her cause has always justified her defiance.

Prologue

I WAS COOKING supper when one of the mothers from the Bristol community telephoned to say that Christopher had been run over outside the kitchen door and had been taken to hospital. I asked her if he was badly hurt and she said the car had knocked him over, run over him and the driver had then panicked and rolled back over his stomach. The ambulance had taken him to hospital. I telephoned the hospital and the nurse said he had died a few minutes before I called. It was one of the bleakest moments of my life.

The whole family got into the car and we drove straight down to the community. The children and the mothers sat at the huge table in the kitchen, some crying, some in white-faced silence. Christopher was dead.

Chris was a thin quiet gentle boy. So rarely do we get a gentle boy of thirteen at Chiswick Women's Aid that I was determined to move him with his mother and two sisters from the central refuge down to this particular community house that is my own extended family. His mother had come into the central refuge for battered wives with her three children not only because her husband was repeatedly violent towards her but also because he beat and tormented Christopher, who was highly intelligent and gentle and therefore a constant irritation to his alcoholic shiftless father. Philomena, his ten-year-old sister, was diabetic and epileptic and Margaret, the younger girl, was cowed and silent. Eileen, the mother, had constantly tried to get help for herself and the children. Philomena had spent years in hospital. Chris was treated by the same hospital for migraine and Eileen for depression, but no one would tackle the source of the problem—the father.

When the family arrived at the refuge we were so overcrowded that we had put up two large garden sheds at the bottom of the

---

garden. Though the sheds had no lighting or heating we had made them as attractive as possible, and the larger one held twelve mothers and children. We were able to fit Eileen and her children into a gap left by a mother on her way to a new life in one of our satellite community homes. Eileen soon settled in spite of the noise and confusion of the huge refuge, because she knew she was safe and was surrounded by people who would love and care for her. The two girls began to make friends, but I was very worried about Chris. He was so depressed that he rarely moved from the shed. He would sit on the bed for hours writing about death and suicide. He never smiled and rarely spoke to anyone. The other children of all ages laughed and played, but Chris seemed unable to accept their overtures. I spent hours sitting and talking to him with members of the play-group staff. Slowly he unbent and we could see him walking around the garden wearing a shabby grey mac which he never took off. Meanwhile, Philomena was having trouble with her diabetes, which meant frequent trips to hospital, but there were no epileptic fits. The little family was getting on its feet. Christopher found that all the mothers liked him, put their arms around him and gently teased him, and he began to smile. He had a very small face masked by a huge pair of glasses and could usually be found in a corner of the sitting-room deep in a book.

Because by law children must attend school, Christopher was placed at Chiswick Comprehensive. The staff there have always been very understanding with our children, but on his first day Christopher collapsed, and they were alarmed because for a few minutes his heart completely stopped beating. We decided that Christopher should stay in the security of the refuge until we were able to move him into a more permanent setting. The doctor assured me that he did not have anything organically wrong but that years of beating and verbal abuse had taken their toll of this shy sensitive boy, and it would take a long time to undo the damage. I was confident that we could undo it, and the day came when they were ready to move to Bristol.

The house at Bristol had been going for some time. It was used as one of our settled communities where five mothers and their children could live together for a period of time while they recovered from the dreadful damage inflicted on them by the violent men they lived with, and began to look towards a new future. When I first saw the house, long before we moved into it, it had been empty for many years; once it must have been magnificent. John Pontin, who was a property developer, asked me if I wanted it for our mothers and children. Sitting on the grass in the sun, I fell in love with the big shabby house and could hear the sounds of future children laughing and playing in the large generous rooms. On the way back to the house, from the long grass that grew round the front porch, I picked up an old-fashioned pair of spectacles with half-lenses. They had probably belonged to the old vicar who had last lived in the house, and I felt it was a good omen: I took them home.

It took much longer to buy the house than John expected, and when I was finally told it was ours I was also warned that vandals had been in. By this time there were about 125 mothers and children at the central refuge, sleeping in ten rooms and the two sheds. Several families had been in Chiswick for some months and were ready to move on. These were families that had suffered such violence that there was no hope of them ever returning to their own homes. Though the courts would evict their husbands and hand the houses back to the wives, the danger of the men returning to batter or even kill the mothers and children was far too great and the mothers knew they would have to make a new life elsewhere under assumed names.

The first family I chose for the Bristol house was Maureen, with her two children, Mark and Kim. She had spent sixteen years with a man who had beaten her, knifed her, put a poker through her jaw and stubbed cigarettes out on her chest. His violence extended to the children not only in immediate explosions of rage but also in cruel sadistic jokes when he would make them eat slices of bread thickly spread with hot mustard, or would put 50p into Mark's hand and turn him out into the night, telling him to look for his 'real' father. He would take a great delight in torturing Maureen, forcing Mark to watch him, revelling in the little boy's helplessness. He would hang her screaming and naked upside down over the balcony on the ninth storey of a block of flats and Mark would desperately hang on to her, crying and pleading for him not to let her go. Bored with that game he would pull her back, beat her up and slam out to the pub. The two children would clean up the blood and débris and comfort her, and she would again go down to the Welfare and ask for help. They did once put her into a bed-and-breakfast a few streets away from where they lived, but as the husband was a dustman by trade, they spent most of the few days crouched on the floor of the little room fearing with every dust cart that went past that they would be found. Eventually they went back because the fear of the violence was worse than the violence.

By this time Mark was seriously violent. At eight he was very fat and very strong. At school the teachers were so wary of his exploding rage that they would not dare to ask Mark to leave the classroom. They just removed the rest of the class and left him undisturbed. He was also beginning to learn that violence pays. One day he threatened his teacher with a knife and they at last referred him to a day hospital for treatment. At this same hospital Maureen had a record stretching back for years: pages of evidence which read like a horror story. There was also a record with the local authority which started when she herself was a little girl and was in and out of children's homes when her own mother was so badly beaten she could not carry on. She remembered her father too drunk to walk, crawling on his hands and knees towards his house where his terrified wife and children waited. The violence in both Maureen's and her husband's cases can be traced back five generations.

After the day when a nurse at the hospital put a scrap of paper into Maureen's hand on which was written '369 Chiswick High Road', the biggest challenge for us at the refuge was to see whether we could save Mark from becoming a man who would batter and whether Kim, his sister, might grow up to marry a man who was not violent.

Pat with her two little boys were the next family to be sent to the Bristol community. She had arrived at the refuge when a huge donation of clothing was piled on the floor of the sitting-room. Mothers were rummaging like lunatics. Within minutes her few possessions were gone and this upset her far more than the noise and the confusion. Pat was a fierce independent woman of twenty-five. She had a son, Daniel, who was six, and Jason, aged four. Daniel took about ten minutes to sort out the other little boys but Jason stayed close to her. Pat's husband had been released from Broadmoor where he had been imprisoned for attacking a warder.

Because he was always violent and murderous in his rage, Pat had made a run for it to us, and because the new community house at Bristol would need so much energy to get it on its feet, I asked her if she would like to go. We needed her organizing ability.

The third mother to go to Bristol was Noela, with her son Peter. Noela was a state registered nurse, but when she came to the refuge I didn't think we could do anything to help her. She had been in mental hospitals so many times and had been treated so often with ECT that she would lie in the foetal position on the sofa burbling and rambling, oblivious of everyone. Peter was a skinny aggressive little nine-year-old. He was rude and tormenting to his mother. He was a complete outsider in the refuge; a wide range of behaviour was tolerated there, but he was personally so insulting to everyone that he was hated. However, little by little he began to tell me about his father, who was a clever man with a good education and a degree, but so badly damaged himself that he was unable to keep a job and would drink until he came home having wet and soiled himself, demanding that Peter and his mother clean up the trail he had left behind him. He would often beat his wife and then rape her, and Peter hearing her screaming would rush into the bedroom and watch helplessly until his father was spent and rolled over into a deep drunken sleep. Every time Noela was beaten unconscious and taken to hospital she was diagnosed as 'depressive' and passed on to the psychiatric unit, where they used ECT and then returned her more confused, more desperate and less able to cope. Peter had got to the stage where he hated his mother because he felt she couldn't rescue him from this intolerable situation, and he despised her mindless rambling and inability to think coherently. There was a clear danger that Peter was going to take over the father's role of sadistic bully; he was observed by the staff hitting and kicking Noela when he was frustrated. I felt that the energy and common sense of Pat and Maureen might pull her through and it was worth trying. Even before she left the central refuge she was becoming much more aware of everything around her and had begun to consider her appearance—though she looked pitifully thin, as she weighed only 5½ stone.

The fourth family was June and her two boys. June was a teacher. The clever child of her own family, carrying on her shoulders the dreams and ambitions of an intelligent under-educated mother, she had married a black youth worker, not realizing until it was much too late that he was violent. He beat her and used sticks and belts on the boys. When she came into the refuge she had a swollen chin and a split lip. She had spent two days locked in the house holding the lip together in an attempt to get it to heal. Finally the husband had relaxed his guard and she was able to bolt with the two boys. I had originally put her into the first community house we opened, at the other end of Chiswick, but her husband hearing that she was in the Chiswick area began to tour round carrying photos of her and the boys, showing them to the milkmen and other children playing in the street. He was seen at the end of the road near the community house and we then knew he had found her. On a bank holiday Monday when all the mothers and children from the central refuge as well as from the community house in Chiswick had gone to Southend, a fire swept through the top floor of the newly renovated and decorated community. It started in June's room and took the roof off. Weeks of hard work went up in smoke and everything June had managed to accumulate had gone. It seemed necessary to move her and her boys, so they went with the other families to Bristol.

When they arrived in our dilapidated old van they found to their horror that not only had the vandals smashed every pane of glass, but thieves had totally denuded the house of every bit of piping. The electric cables had been ripped out and the lavatory smashed. They telephoned me and asked if they should come back to London. I said no. With the four mothers and myself, we would be able to put it all into shape again. After all, we were all capable women, and at that time the public were still generously sending in donations and we had saved sufficient to buy beds, temporary lighting and blankets. So they stayed on. I came down with my children for the weekend, bringing a large bottle of wine. We cooked a celebration meal for all of us and toasted the future.

I said many prayers for that house, and one day a young woman telephoned me and said she would like to give me some money. Imagining it would be a generous donation of £25, I was delighted and asked her round. When she was seated with a cup of coffee in her hand she asked me what I would do if I were given quite a large sum of money. I explained many of my hopes for the future, including getting this new community on its feet. She liked the sound of that scheme best and she began to write out a cheque. The suspense was unbearable. When I looked at it it read '£10,000'. She had inherited this sum and did not believe in taking money for which she had not worked. I have never seen her again but the house stands as a tribute to her generosity.

By the time Eileen arrived in Bristol several of the mothers had moved on. Pat had happily remarried, a very nice gentle man, June had got a good job teaching and found her own accommodation, and Maureen and Noela were still there. There were two other mothers with their children well settled in and quite happy. The house was nearly finished. We had run out of money because the roof required vast sums spent on it, but hours of hard work and a good building firm meant that we were warm and comfortable.

I drove Eileen and her three down to Bristol, with my own children who loved staying in the community. When we parked our car outside the back door that Friday night and hooted twice, as we always did, the children of the community poured out to kiss us and the mothers came out to help with the luggage. I remember how bewildered Eileen and the children looked standing in the kitchen. To us a kitchen shared by five mothers and some fourteen children is chaos, but Eileen had just left a kitchen at the central refuge shared by forty-five mothers and sixty-five children, so this one seemed very quiet. We all sat down to a community meal and then Eileen put the two girls to bed in her own room and Chris shared a big room with two other boys. While we were drinking coffee Eileen burst into tears and we all understood why she was crying, and reassured her. Most mothers when they leave the central refuge miss the great warmth and excitement of a busy industrious community. It takes a while to settle down in any of the smaller communities.

I left them settling into a new life and drove back to London worrying about Christopher, who had regressed again to wandering round the house wearing his old mac. But I needn't have worried, because by the next weekend he was joining in the conversation at the table. Gradually as the children included him in their lives and the mothers made friends with him he grew visibly brighter and brighter. A few weekends later we arrived hot and tired from a hard week's work. We walked into the kitchen and to our delight and amazement there was Chris without his mac, shyly trying to copy the other children who were dancing the 'bump'. It was like a miracle. I looked at my husband and we smiled. It was an awkward stilt-like performance but he was trying, and then he saw us and smiled a big happy smile and we all laughed and the whole kitchen danced.

After that day Chris never stopped—he drove everyone mad with the gramophone and he learnt all the latest dances. He settled into his new school but he would come home during his dinner hour and dance all by himself in the big kitchen, oblivious to the mothers wandering in and out, just happy to have discovered the music.

One day Maureen was at the kitchen stove and asked Chris to go to the 'chippy' for her. He dashed out of the kitchen and 'tapped' one of the boys as he went. It was a signal for a game of tag and he shot out of the kitchen door straight under a car that was driving very slowly up our side of the road. He should not have died. The car was only doing ten miles an hour, but the driver panicked and the damage was terminal. He lay in the road for half an hour before the ambulance came. The community knelt with him. Maureen held his hands and when he found it difficult to breath from his crushed chest she said the two-times table with him. He kept saying 'Don't let me die' and they all reassured him, but he did die and it was probably the only time so far that my faith in God has ever wavered. That he should be happy for a bare seven or eight weeks of his life and then die, and that he should have to suffer so badly before he died seemed like a total betrayal of my belief in a loving God. The only consolation I could offer Eileen was that the community loved and cared for her and her children and we would always remember her son.

The mothers and staff of the central refuge came down for the funeral. The social worker working with Christopher's father, who was being treated at yet another hospital for depression, insisted that the father should be at the funeral. Though Eileen dreaded seeing him, the social worker, backed by the man's family, said he had his rights. I felt that although it was another burden on Eileen, if the husband who had lost everything he had by his violent behaviour—his home, his wife, his daughters, and finally and completely his

son—wanted to come, we should try and make the funeral as dignified an event as possible.

It was dignified. When we all saw Christopher's father so heavily
drugged that he had to be supported by his two sisters, we all felt
sorry for him. He was a big, thick-set, bewildered-looking man. Born
and raised in violence, he had had little opportunity to live any other
kind of life. As he stood at Christopher's grave the tears rolled down
his face; at least if he was unable to show any love for Christopher
while he was alive, he had a chance to mourn for him now he was
dead. I feel Chris would have been pleased that his dad had come,
for, however cruel and violent the men are, the children still care
for them.

The mothers took Eileen back to the house and looked after her
and cared for her while she slowly recovered. The funeral had
shaken me badly because the last funeral I had attended was my
mother's, and the only people there had been my father, his sisters,
my twin sister and my brother.

ONE

China, South Africa, Beirut

IT HAS ALWAYS seemed strange to me that I am unable to recall any dates in my childhood. I have absolutely no memory of when events occurred, merely a kaleidoscopic jumble of things that happened. But I know, because I have my birth certificate, when I was born: in 1939 in Tsingtao in China.

My mother, who was Canadian, nearly died giving birth to me and my twin sister, a fact neither parent ever forgave us for and which perhaps fostered the feeling of personal responsibility for the misfortunes of others that has haunted me all my life. Once we were safely delivered, she handed us over to the nursery staff which occupied a wing of the mock-castle my parents rented, and went off to visit her friends in Shanghai.

The staff of the nursery consisted of the obligatory English nanny and two Chinese amahs. Almost my first memory is of furiously pedalling my tricycle down a cobbled street in an attempt to catch up with one of the amahs who had just been dismissed by my mother. The hiring and firing of those people who were there to care for me continued throughout my young life, and my recurring nightmare is running down a road with hands outstretched, pursuing a fleeing figure which is part nanny, part mother, but always elusive.

It may seem heartless of my mother to have handed my sister and me over to a sterile nursery regime; but you have to realize that her own mother had died when she was two years old. She was sent to live with an elderly childless couple, relations of the family who were comfortably off, and grew up a lonely, isolated little girl. The fantasy world which she created to make her childhood bearable stayed with her all her life, and to this day I am discovering that stories and situations which in my own childhood I believed to be true were total fabrication.

Infernal Child

When she left school she went to Toronto to study medicine. She was hopelessly shy and very rarely went out with boys; if one called on her she usually retreated under the bed (or so she said) until the boy was shooed away. She qualified as a nurse at the time of the great depression in Canada. The paper mills owned by the elderly couple who had brought her up failed at this time, and in an effort to earn a living she applied for a job in a large hospital in Peking. She got the job and set sail for China with a lot of matching luggage and no worldly experience at all.

The 'princess' is the most dangerous of the female species. Men always fall in love with her beautiful childlike qualities. My mother was only five foot two, with thick auburn hair; her eyes were a vivid blue, and she had a surprisingly beautiful deep musical voice. It was almost inevitable that this virginal woman with her ingenuous manner would appeal to my father's particular needs. The son of a man with a great reputation, he had a badly scarred, frightened soul. His memories of his Anglo-Irish parents were very bitter.

I once saw a photograph of my paternal grandfather: his shoulders stretched right across the picture. He had a broad Irish face and the look of a man who was never far from trouble. He is said to have drunk a quart of whisky a day, and to have been able to hold five men against the wall with one arm. He had a passion for horses; when he couldn't afford to race them he bought a team of them to haul coal round the neighbourhood. Later he became a policeman, and still later he moved into a large pub, partly as another business venture, but also because he needed to house his seventeen children. My father remembered dancing on the bar to entertain the public.

He had nothing to say about his mother, whom he hated and who ended up in a mental hospital. All I know about her is that she weighed 17 stone and that I was supposed to be like her. I always understood that my grandmother was really the more powerful of the two, and that my father was much more frightened of her than of my grandfather, who was unpredictable but lovable. I was not at all upset when my father warned me of my resemblance to his mother, as I always fancied being a big powerful woman in a world where normal-sized women are obviously at a disadvantage except in certain well-defined fields.

It must have taken great determination for my father, the seventeenth child of his parents, to work his way through school, take a commission in the Air Force then move across to become a captain in the Army, and finally to come out top in the Civil Service exams. He was in the diplomatic service in China when he met and married my mother. She had meanwhile inherited quite a lot of money from her guardians, and with this money they sailed round the world on their honeymoon, accompanied by forty cabin trunks, all with matching covers. On their return they set up house together in Shanghai.

In those days the diplomatic corps in the Far East enjoyed a standard of luxury they were never to know again. But while the Germans, the French and the English were drinking champagne, collecting porcelain and travelling through the vast country, the bodies lay piled in the streets and war was approaching. My parents and their friends sided with Chiang Kai-shek. One day the Japanese marched into Shanghai and the long party was over. Taken hostage, we were lucky enough to be exchanged for Japanese prisoners-of-war. We sailed on one of the last boats to leave China, on our way to South Africa; many of our friends were sent to prisoner-of-war camps in Manila and elsewhere.

My twin sister and I—she was known as Mei-Mei ('little sister') and I as Chei-Chei ('older sister')—were three and a half. I remember almost nothing of the boat journey but my mother told us that the Japanese guards took a great fancy to the two little English girls. They gave us fresh fruit and as a special treat they would take us down to the hold where we would watch the beating and torturing which was part of the entertainment of the crew.

When we arrived in South Africa we were refugees in a strange country. My mother lived with us two toddlers in a small bungalow, while my father went off to join a diplomatic mission in Beirut. I remember very little of that time except for a very fat black nanny who took us to school every day and allowed us to ride on her back while she scrubbed the floor. She was a deeply superstitious woman and one day as we ambled along the road on the way to school we passed a huge boulder with a little wizened black man squatting precariously on the top. Smoke was seeping out of the base of the rock and I laughed uproariously, pointing at him and shouting. The nanny grabbed me by the arm, putting her hand over my mouth, and dragged me away but not before the man shouted that he would come and see me that night. His manner was so prophetic that I was afraid. The nanny told me that he was a holy man who had been commanded by the village to sit on top of the rock to propitiate the gods for the soul of an eagle which had been killed by accident and was now being burned. I had committed a dreadful offence by laughing at him. She muttered all the way to school.

I told my mother, who paid no attention, but that night I lay petrified in the bedroom we all three shared. In the early hours of the morning my sister insisted on going to the lavatory, accompanied by my mother. I begged to go with them but my mother was firm: I was to stay in my bed. I lay with my back to the window and my hands over my face. Then I heard his voice outside calling my name. I turned over and there in the moonlight at the window was a face in profile. It was silvered, whether or not by moonlight I couldn't decide. And the voice spoke to me. I covered my ears, then, but it left such a strong impression that I am always drawn to any South African I meet, believing that one day someone from there will tell me what the voice was saying all those years ago—probably 'Beware Hounslow Council'.

When, eventually, we joined my father in Beirut, we lived in a block of flats in the middle of the teeming city. I was old enough by that time to be horrified by the beggars and the starving children staring at us with empty hopeless eyes every time we went out. Immediately my sister and I began raiding the food supplies in our kitchen and carrying down everything we could lay our hands on to give to the queue of beggars outside the front door. But our largesse lasted only twenty-four hours, because my mother discovered the plundered kitchen and was even more appalled to see the huge crowd waiting for us the next morning. It was explained to us in the best middle-class terms that it was pointless for us to encourage the beggars—they were so numerous that nothing could be done to alleviate their misery, and besides, most of them were layabouts and wastrels who maimed their children in order to obtain money and food. I was sceptical of this explanation.

In Beirut we were quickly enrolled in a local school and kept well occupied. However, during all the years I lived in the Middle

East I was never able to come to terms with the suffering of the people which contrasted so sharply with the way we lived with our servants and cars. My father, while shovelling costly food and wine down his throat, would recount stories of his deprived childhood: of holes in his shoes, lack of food, treks to school with his bum exposed through his unpatched britches. He was quite oblivious of the fact that our servants were expected to bring up their children under much the same conditions. I realized that for many people, to be employed by foreigners at least guaranteed them an income; but I found it incomprehensible that the woman who bathed me, sang to me and put me to bed couldn't eat with me, particularly when my sister and I shared the evening meal with our parents who were so obviously bored with us.

Beirut was a very beautiful city. The cedars of Lebanon, apart from giving shade and smelling of resin, were a hunting ground for sweet white-kernelled nuts, and the hills outside the city were yellow with mimosa. Diplomatic social life ebbed and flowed, and most evenings our parents were out and about at cocktail parties and dinners. Often I would watch our own flat fill up with beautifully dressed Frenchwomen and their husbands. Even then, though I was very young, I could distinguish between the style and elegance of the French and the slightly dumpy austerity of our English guests. My sister and I were supposed to go round the room dropping small curtsies to the women and shaking hands with the men. We were there to be looked it, but apart from a chance remark no one paid any attention to us because children just didn't figure in adult lives except as possessions.

I was fast becoming a deviant and rude little girl. Banned from a children's party for some misdemeanour—it could have been at the request of the hostess—I arrived dressed only in my knickers, spat in the good lady's face, shouted the word *shit* (in French) several times and returned home. Any attention I could get was better than none and it had become obvious to me that the only way to attract any sort of concern from my otherwise-occupied parents was to outrage their sensibilities. Inspired by the success of my tactics I continued to rampage through the homes and lives of many bewildered and uncomprehending adults.

I could read fluently from an early age and I read voraciously, preferring stories wreathed in sulphur from the Norse gods rather than the reading books we were given at school. The school was a strict French convent and we were the only English children there, but we were expected to cope even though we were unable to speak a word of French. Of course we learned to speak French quite quickly and to fit in with the formal discipline at the school. Many of the children there were orphans and they were expected to spend long hours embroidering table linen and napkins to be sold to pay for their keep. My mother bought some of these but I could never look at the exquisite pieces of material without seeing the pricked and callused hands of my friends who had to sit hour after hour bent over their enforced labour.

My mother's taste for fine things, preferably hand-made, was one she indulged constantly no matter where we were. She had a marvellous phrase, *'bonne bouche'* . . . loosely translated it means something good for the mouth. My father would arrive clutching a huge bill in one hand and his head in the other. This was a cue for her immediately to comfort herself, after the horrid reality of a bill for hand-blocked linen ordered from Ireland, with a large present usually from Harrods. If she happened to be at the other end of the world, it made the *bonne bouche* rather expensive. This particular habit has been handed on to me and I am afraid my immediate response to any unpleasing incident is to retire to a hot bath with an ice-cold bottle of Dom Perignon.

When my sister and I were between five and six, my mother announced that she was pregnant. She had always made it clear to us that she desperately wanted a boy. My father's comment on hearing the news, which seemed to come as a total surprise to him, was that it was going to cost him a lot of money. This reduced my mother to tears. To us our father was always frightening and bois-terous. We never knew if his jocular tone was genuine or would turn from a malicious teasing to an angry outburst, so we were very wary.

During the heat of the Lebanese summer we joined other families up in the mountains while the men stayed in the city. I remember it as a time of freedom because the children ran wild, rarely coming into contact with adults. The servants took care of our practical needs and the parents continued to visit each other and play bridge.

Infernal Child

We were in the mountains when my mother went into hospital to have the baby. I was playing on the top bunk in my room clutching a lethal old dagger that was my prize possession. As I stepped on to the ladder I missed my grip on it and fell, landing my head on the stone floor.

I was very badly concussed but my father would not let them take me to hospital in case it would worry my mother who was giving birth. We always came a very poor second to the passion my father felt for his child bride. Even though he tormented my mother he loved her deeply, and never really accepted his luck in owning something so beautiful and precious. (My mother, on the other hand, never loved anything very much except for short bursts, and then it was far more likely to be a painting or a piece of ivory.) I was very ill after my fall, but being virtually indestructible I recovered.

When my mother returned home with my brother Danny it was soon clear how much she loved him. We were all dreadfully jealous of him. I remember looking at him lying in her arms and bursting into tears. Mother laughed at me because I said he was ugly but I was really crying because I had no memory of ever being held or cuddled by her. The most contact she allowed all her life was a kiss on the cheek on the way to bed.

Perhaps my jealousy of Danny was greater because by this time I was old enough to observe that boys had a far freer, easier life than girls. Dolls, dresses and girlish pastimes bored me and I spent my time with the boys playing cowboys and trying to pee standing up. Contrary to popular opinion, provided you wait till you have a full bladder it is perfectly possible. Also, about that time, my first real boyfriend decided to initiate me into the delights of making babies. We found an empty room and removed our clothes, only to be disturbed by my inquisitive sister whom we invited to join us. But once unclothed and astride me, fully confident of his information, John found he had run out of ideas. Rather than allow his frail ego to wilt, I informed him that the proper thing to do was to pee into an available cup which was then to be drunk by my sister. This idea captivated us both as extremely symbolic though the hardship to my sister, who complied though resentfully, was long remembered.

TWO

North America

OUR FAMILY SEEMED to move constantly, but I don't remember ever being consulted about it; my parents never sat down with us and told us what was to happen or where we were to go. One day the packing cases simply arrived, filled with musty straw, and we knew it was time to move again. Tiny little men who looked the same the world over would arrive and start wrapping everything in sight in newspaper. Day by day the house would get barer, until finally a large car drew up and we would get in and drive off to a train or a boat or an aeroplane.

This time it was goodbye to Beirut: we were on our way to America.

Chicago in wartime was an impossible place. There was no rented accommodation to be found anywhere, and most hotels only allowed a five-day stay. We had to move about like gypsies. I remember my sister and me sitting bolt upright, screaming with fear, in our hotel beds 24 floors up from the dining room where our parents sat eating dinner. What had frightened us is unclear—probably my horrific ghost stories—but the next morning the newspapers reported that the dismembered body of a small child had been found in the basement of our hotel. After that we took turns staying awake guarding each other.

I suppose it never occurred to either of our parents that we might be afraid in a strange hotel in a strange country. They had both been uncared for as children and if challenged now by another adult would have been genuinely perplexed. We were warm, fed and financially safe, so why the fuss? I have often found that parents who have been described as uncaring or neglectful are really hurt when faced with this charge, as they cannot identify with the fear or pain of the child they have damaged.

Damaged and roving children retain very little detail from what happens to them, except the incidents that strain their ability to survive. That must be why what I particularly remember about Chicago is that it was where I learned my mother was under sentence of death. She was suffering from the fatal Hodgkin's disease, my father told us; and as new lumps were appearing on her neck she was just waiting the doctors' verdict on how long she had to live. He also pointed out that my sister had been born with the same sort of glands, and so he imagined would suffer the same fate.

My father's preoccupation with death must have stemmed from the appalling scenes he had witnessed as a child, when so many of his brothers and sisters died very young. He told us of hours spent kneeling at the bedside of some small child choking its life away with diphtheria. Nothing had been spared him as a child and he was unable to spare us. This time he was wrong, as it happened : my mother did not have the dreadful disease. But from that point onwards I always had the feeling that my mother was not well, and I lived in fear of her dying.

In Los Angeles, our next port of call, we seemed to stay for months in a boarding house, but once again my memories are fragmentary. I remember a particularly unpleasant little girl who refused to lend me her bike, and in order to make sure I didn't get it she tied it up with string in the garage. I got into the garage when it was quite dark and an elderly man shuffled towards me. 'Do you love me?' he asked, smiling a gummy smile. 'Of course I do,' I said and flung my lonely arms around him. I suppose my enthusiastic response must have taken him by surprise, for he asked me to shut my eyes, then turn round and feel something for him. I didn't like what I felt and broke free. I ran to my mother and told her that there was an old man in the garage who had a snake that would bite me. She was quick on the uptake, though she said nothing much to me. I heard the next day from my friends that the police had arrived and taken the old man back to a mental home. I remember feeling very sorry for him and puzzled that my mother did not wish to pursue the matter of the snake any further.

An old man with a hungry mouth, a flaccid penis, the police, a crying mother and a ranting father are a not-unfamiliar pattern; many young girls have a sexual encounter of this sort in their early childhood. Obviously my mother could not cope with the incident, and rather than quarrel with my father over whose responsibility it was to see I was not allowed to run loose, she left the whole thing to be glossed over. In fact both my parents were abnormally puritanical; even at the age of six or seven my sister and I had never seen a naked adult.

Our stay in Los Angeles was strained, because my father was having the usual personality clashes in his work at the British Consulate. While his ability to write and collate reports was much valued, his explosive and touchy manner made many dislike him. There must have been other tensions as well, for at last he was forced to send us all off to Toronto, where my mother had some good friends.

The friends, Uncle Dick, a pediatrician, and Aunty Elsie, lived in a long and tall house with their several children, including Peter who was a little older than my sister and me, and a spastic. He had been born in a German concentration camp, when Aunty Elsie was so weak it was a miracle either of them survived. The children told us stories of their experiences in the camps and I was fascinated and rather envious of the companionship they all seemed to have enjoyed. Because we had travelled so much and because my father was so anti-social we had few friends, but now that Uncle Dick and Aunty Elsie had invited us to share their house we suddenly had roots. Many old China hands turned up to see us, and I noticed how restless those families seemed. The children spoke of their pets and dolls or played games of Kick the Can. But our gang of 'camp' kids smoked cigarettes behind the shed and reminisced about dead bodies, torture and escape routes, a world that made more sense to me.

My mother had booked us into the best school in the area. On the first day I was sent home with lice. It was an inauspicious start. Once I had been de-infested and returned to school, my mother was summoned once again to explain why I was sexually obsessed. A small group of girls had been seen examining each other at the bottom of the playground. Apparently this had never occurred before, although the girls at that school played very intense, almost non-stop, games of mothers and fathers which the staff considered rather sweet. I had merely taken the game to its logical conclusion in search of facts. The staff were horrified, and I was suspended for some days.

On my return I informed the girls that I had been savagely beaten by my mother. I also handed out several dollars to my friends who, like well-trained sneaks, rushed off to the teacher.

Both the school and my mother were a little desperate by now, and my mother took me home and put me on the doorstep saying that the police were going to come and take me away. My sister stood very loyally beside me. She had learned a long time ago to watch and say nothing, and we remained there until late at night, waiting for the dreadful moment to arrive. Finally my mother relented and we were allowed to go to bed. A few weeks later she found me sitting on the bottom step outside the house handing out her housekeeping money to passers-by. This time she lost control completely and beat me with the flex of the iron.

The beating left indelible scars on me because all the time I knew that the stealing, the lying and the anti-social behaviour were desperate pleas for love. She couldn't see this, or that the stealing was so I could give to others. Slowly I shut myself off from her. She began to congratulate herself on my improved behaviour, but even if I now looked and behaved the same as others, my feelings had changed. Somewhere deep down I had decided it was too painful to live. I decided to kill off my inner self, never to allow it to feel anything deeply again.

My mother soon got bored with Toronto and with living on her own, without my father, in someone else's house. She began to go off on long visits, taking my brother with her. I don't remember that she made any attempt to explain; it was just understood that we would remain where we were, like small abandoned parcels, and eventually she would return as full of enthusiasm and as enchanting as ever.

My memories of Canada seem to centre around huge parklands and playing spaces. For much of the time Aunty Elsie shooed us out of the house, and on one particularly cold, snowy afternoon a group of six of us were sent off to go tobogganing. I stood at the top of the steep slope watching hundreds of children and adults hurtling down. There was no way I was going to risk life and limb following my friends down, so I loitered about until I got thoroughly cold and then decided I would walk home. I started off quite cheerfully but soon realized that I was lost. The banks of snow along the sidewalks were towering above my head. I had not known, never having experienced much snow before, that when the roads and sidewalks were cleared it was like walking down a long tunnel, the houses just above the banks being obscured. As I grew more tired and frightened, the freezing cold crept into my bones and I felt as though I needed to sleep. I must have fallen sideways into a pile of snow and without realizing it I was dying. Forever after I knew that dying was a happy experience. I slipped into a warm comfortable dreaming state. If this is what dying is about, I thought to myself, I don't mind at all.

I awoke in great agony with hard human hands rubbing my feet and trying to comfort me. I was screaming with pain as my frozen body slowly restored itself to life. Totally bewildered, I didn't know who I was or where I lived. I knew my mother had gone again and all I wanted was my doll, called Chei-Chei (like me). This moth-eaten, cloth-bodied, lumpy creature with a china head had been given me in Shanghai and though I beat her badly she was the one constant thing in my life and I loved her. The family that rescued me finally tracked down Uncle Dick and Aunty Elsie who came to pick me up. I was taken back to the long, tall house which now felt like a prison. In disgrace once again, I sat on the old-fashioned radiator shivering while the family sat down to their evening meal at the far end of the room, ignoring me.

My mother's friends who were looking after us must have got very fed up with all the cuts, bruises, and near-catastrophes that interrupted their smooth-running routine, for I was dreadfully accident-prone. In order to learn to take care of himself the child has first to be taken care of. If he lacks mothering as I did, the child never internalizes the warning mother's voice or the cautionary arms which act as an unconscious guide. There is a cardboard quality about him: as he is never cuddled or stroked, his body becomes merely a casing to be used recklessly. When I put my arms round such children at the refuge, they feel brittle and unyielding, where an emotionally well-mothered child is warm and fits into the contours of the arms round him.

I imagine Uncle Dick and Aunty Elsie must have complained bitterly to my mother when she arrived back, and that is why she decided to take us to visit her brother on his farm near Calgary.

There, to my surprise, we were welcomed. My Aunt Emma was a little warm gentle motherly woman and when I behaved badly she took it in her stride.

There was an old lady who lived up the road from my aunt with whom, for a variety of reasons, I was locked in mortal combat. She had an outside lavatory in a tiny tall shed to which she would retire to relieve herself every morning at ten. One day when she was happily ensconced I tip-toed up and pushed over the shed. It was a major triumph in my war effort. Once she had extracted herself and cleaned up she came storming along the road. I awaited the inevitable explosion with mounting excitement. My heart raced, my mouth was dry and every part of me felt alive.

I stood at the top of the stairs and listened to Aunt Emma calming her down. I was amazed and a little puzzled. Aunt Emma refused to agree that I was a monster who needed shooting—she kept insisting that I needed loving. As her voice didn't rise I couldn't hurl myself downstairs and shout obscenities; she was on my side. The neighbour left. I was bitterly disappointed because I had been cheated of a huge confrontation and such dramas were by now a daily need. I came downstairs wondering if she would react while we were alone. She put her arm around me and gave me a hug. I was very frightened and suspicious of her.

When we sat down to dinner that night everyone had corn on the cob except me. I had the potatoes and vegetables but no corn—a particular treat for which I had been waiting for days. Aunt Emma just said kindly that the old lady was so upset she had given her the corn to make her happy again. Why would Aunt Emma want to make the old bitch happy? It was beyond me, but slowly I found it safe to like her. She knew children. She lived a warm round life on the farm. She saw all problems as both immediate and long-term, so an aggressive act on my part was dealt with immediately but carried with it the loss of something I wanted. Slowly I learned to give up the immediate pleasure of a drama to gain the goal of a hug or kiss of approval, and I settled and do remember moments of great happiness.

The farm had horses, cows and fields of vegetables. It was enormously busy and every morning I lay in bed aware of the movement that ran through the chickens, to the cows standing in the milking shed, across to the horses, round the corn field, and back into the farmyard where the massive hulk of the stud bull rumbled and shook in a permanent mad anger. Everyone got up early and the children left for school on horseback. School was a small clapboard house in the village. The horses were tied outside and all of us bent our heads over the reading, writing and 'rithmetic until it was time to go home. In our absence the day had changed. The electric movement of the morning had died to a still, quiet hum. The cows chewed their cuds, waiting to be milked, and the older boys joined my uncle who would be sitting with a pail between his knees listening to the musical swish of milk filling the bucket. Slowly I became quieter. My sister and I played in the hay barn, found small kittens buried with their mothers and we fell asleep at night in a safe place.

THREE

Teheran

O F C O U R S E M Y mother came back to the farm near Calgary to collect us. I have a faded photograph of my Canadian grandfather who must have come there to see us. He didn't mean anything to me. In the picture my sister looks smaller and stands very seriously beside me.

By then I was so used to moving on that I don't remember how we left Canada; we must have made another long journey by ship. I remember an old oil tanker with a cabin in the stern separated by acres of deck from the front of the ship. The weather was awful and gales howled in the rigging and huge waves washed right over the cabin. There were times when in order to get to the dining room we had to haul ourselves up the almost vertical deck ropes. The cabin was crammed full of hospital beds which lurched and hurled themselves across the room at night; on one occasion, when my mother was too sea-sick to move, the ship's doctor arrived at the door clutching an axe. He had had to keep one hand on the rope and dig the axe into the deck to keep himself from being swept overboard.

It was a nightmare journey but at last we arrived in Persia, where we were to stay for two years. The Embassy in Teheran, where my father was posted, was a large complex of houses surrounded by a long, high wall. At the massive gates were two huge guards with drawn swords who kept up an endless pantomime of saluting and clicking heels as the cars rolled through. The readiness of the salute, like the size of the house one was given, depended on status. But because in the Foreign Office the chauffeur may well be a very senior member of MI5, there was a sense of classless informality among the families living in the compound.

We lived in a middle-sized house close to several other families. It had four bedrooms and several reception rooms and French windows leading into a large garden with a lily pond in the middle. My mother had the pond covered with wire netting because one day while she was resting I threw a huge stone into the pond and raced into the house screaming that my brother had fallen in. I had never seen her move so fast. I was back in my usual embattled role, and for the first time since Beirut we were living again as a family.

In the evening when it was time for my father to return home, I noticed my mother would get flustered. We would hear his loose, phlegmy cough—he smoked nearly a hundred cigarettes a day—and then his key would go into the lock and the door opened. Everyone in the house stopped what they were doing and there would be a silence. If he was smiling we all breathed again, but if he was scowling, his eyes like slits and bloodshot, it would mean that someone had upset him and we were in for trouble. His voice would rise to a nagging whine and he would rage for what seemed like hours.

I never saw him hit my mother but she cried a lot, and their rows were endless. The worst were about money. My father lived on the edge of an imagined abyss of destitution. She lived in the never-never-land of imagined plenty. They were doomed never to meet in the middle. She bought whatever she fancied, usually antiques, paintings or carpets; he saw no reason to buy anything but the basic necessities of life—in fact, it was hard to get him to change his clothes or take a bath as he considered baths weakening. My mother also had a childlike need to keep up with those around her in any social situation. But whenever she arranged a social occasion at our house, with the three children nicely dressed handing round the nuts, my father was bound to do something outrageous and spoil it. Either he would pick an argument with someone and shout, or walk into the room, pick up a newspaper and pretend the place was empty. The guests would then leave. My father usually put on a face of injured innocence and then rowed with my mother for crying. Slowly, as in other places where we had lived, people stopped coming round.

Family meals were tense occasions, for my father, as head of the house, always insisted on his right not only to fill his own plate first with the best food but also to serve us children as he wished. If I was in favour I got a full plate, if not, very little. Even if the meat was embedded in fat I had to eat it, being too afraid to argue. It took me a long time to realize why, years later, I became hysterically aggressive if anyone served food on to a plate for me. Many a dinner party was ruined when the kind host suffered a verbal onslaught at the mere suggestion that I should receive a plate full of spaghetti, before I was able to trace and identify the origin of that phobia. From that moment the anger disappeared, and I can now accept other people serving my food.

In Teheran my sister and I attended the American School, a huge place with children from all the Embassies; rich Persian families sent their children there to learn English. My sister did very well there but I was always in trouble. I couldn't write very well and my spelling was bizarre. It was long before anyone realized that such defects can come from a form of word-blindness, so I was often punished for being lazy. The teacher was an American woman who shouted furiously at me and hit my knuckles with a large ruler till they were swollen and puffy. She satisfied all my needs for excitement and drama and I disrupted the classroom and the playground with great success. In the photograph of our class of about forty children, the back three rows are girls, neatly braided and smiling. The front two rows are the boys sprawling and in the middle of the front row I am also sprawling. I earned my position in that row by being one of the worst fighters in the class. I was unable to feel pain when I was angry, and would attempt to kill anyone I fought with. The other children had limits beyond which they would not go but I would simply go on until I became exhausted. My sister too was violent, but only when provoked and in defence of me. Otherwise she remained quiet and well behaved, though she was plagued with eczema.

Across the road from the school was a shop that sold comics. I had an insatiable passion for reading, but there were few books in our house, or in any of the Embassy houses, because everyone travelled so much, so that that shop crammed with thick American comics was a paradise. You bought your first few comics and then sold them back to the shop at half price and bought more. I bought my comics regularly and talked cheerfully to the man who ran the shop. One day he stood behind me and, putting his hands on my shoulders, began to rub himself up and down my back. I stood still and surprised. After a few minutes he stopped making a panting noise, breathed deeply and picked up a large bundle of comics and gave them to me. I was delighted. I took them home, read them all and took them back. Because the shop was full he took me into the next room. More heavy breathing, rubbing up and down, and another pile of comics. I knew perfectly well that this was somehow wrong. Although my only sexual experience had been with the old man in the garage in Los Angeles, I could sense the urgent need I aroused in this man and realized that I had the power to supply myself with comics whenever I felt like it.

Unfortunately I told a friend of mine, and she then repeated it to my mother, who grabbed me by the hand and marched me off to the shop. The man denied the whole incident and insisted that I had stolen the comics. They reached a stalemate because my mother said she was going to report him to the police for molesting a child; he was going to report me to the police for stealing the comics. They stood there glaring at each other while I stood meekly behind her indignant back regretting my loss of reading matter.

I never learned what she felt about the whole affair because there was no discussion between us. All that happened was that I was removed from the school, partly because of the proximity of the shop and partly because the school thought it would be a good idea, as I was too disruptive. So a tutor was found, a splendid round dumpling of a lady who taught me to sing 'I am S.A.V.E.D.' and other such evangelical songs. She would then spend the rest of the day trying to find me. The grounds of the Embassy compound were huge and I could always find a tree up which I could disappear until dark.

In the compound were beautiful lily ponds like the one in our garden; the water in them was dark and muddy and the huge leaves lay flatly on the water. All the children were warned to stay away from these pools but we didn't listen. One day I pushed one of the smaller girls in because she had annoyed me, and while the others ran for help I watched her sink and come up again. The first time she came up her face was contorted and shouting, the second time her mouth was round and made no sound, and the third time just her face surfaced: it was resigned and smooth, her eyes and her mouth peaceful. Then help arrived. But I didn't join in because I was too busy watching. I didn't feel that her drowning cries and her struggle had anything to do with me. The other mothers told my mother I was dangerous. She told me I was dangerous. I knew I was dangerous, but how could I cope with myself?

One morning when I was avoiding my tutor I found a bird's nest with about six blue, speckled eggs in it. I cracked one and saw inside a tiny naked bird. The baby bird was not yet ready to hatch, but its eyes were alive and its beak opened and shut. The beak was so huge in its skeletal domed head that the baby seemed to be smiling ridiculously. I broke open all the eggs and arranged the tiny babies in a row on a big rock. I sat crouched beside them with a long piece of straw, tickling them to see them move, until one by one they died. I was fascinated by that experience. I also found huge green grasshoppers whose legs I would pull off and watch while their jewelled eyes slowly dimmed.

Then in my lonely wanderings I found a puppy. It was round, black and whimpering in a ditch. I took it home and begged my mother to let me keep it and she agreed. I called the puppy Bageera and because he was so grateful to me for saving him he began to respond. It didn't matter to him if I hit him; he crouched and implored me not to do it again. Wherever I went he followed. His fat, eager behind shaking with love, he would creep into my bed at night and lie close beside me, and in the morning he would roll his eyes with ecstasy and lick my face before creeping downstairs. We became friends and I was able to be gentle with him. So much total loving is healing. Then he caught distemper. My mother realized how frantic I was and let me stay with him while his eyes ran with mucus and his chest bubbled and wheezed. As he got weaker and weaker I fed him with a dropper. I lay all night beside him praying for his life and he watched me with hope. One night I felt his body shudder under my hand. He looked very intensely at me and then died. I buried him in the garden and after that, because I had discovered the possibility of love without the danger I found in relationships with human beings, I began to collect animals.

The local drivers of the Embassy cars knew my dog had died and one of them brought me a gazelle which had been abandoned by its mother. I was delighted with this beautiful, elegant creature and carried her home, where she immediately settled into her role as a family pet. Unfortunately she was totally un-house-trained and when she felt playful she would leap around the furniture, over the tables and chairs, crash up and down the corridors and dent the walls with her sharp little hooves. In about a week she had ploughed up the garden and eaten all the plants. She loved cigarettes, and would demolish any packet of them my father absent-mindedly put down. So he began to object to the gazelle, and a new home was found for her. I kissed her goodbye on her soft whiskery muzzle, promising I would come to see her, but I never did see her again because she ate her owner's silk stockings and choked to death.

My mother was remarkably good about my animals, partly because she genuinely liked them, but also because she was pleased I had at last found something with which to occupy myself. When another driver arrived with a meat-hawk, a huge fierce bird with a broken wing, my mother and I decided to look after it. I fed it raw meat while she used her medical experience to splint the wing. When she had finished I chained it to a perch in the kitchen and it looked around quite happy and content. It stayed with me until the wing healed, and it gradually regained the strength to fly. For a while it would merely fly up in a tree and sit. If anyone came into the garden they had to remember to wear a heavy leather glove and to stretch out an arm, or they would find themselves skewered suddenly by the talons of the bird as it arrived heavily on their shoulders. One day the hawk flew away and I was happy for it. I swore that I would be a vet, but before I could collect any more animals we moved from Teheran up to the Suma compound, about an hour's drive from the city.

It was a much better compound for the children. Here we had a huge old house with a wide veranda and a big garden. The servants' quarters, which I always checked first whenever we moved because it was there that we would spend most of our time, were at the back, separated from the main house. The compound itself was much less formally organized than the one in the city. There were acres of wild vegetation around it and although the Ambassador's summer residence stood magnificently in the centre of the compound, there was no formal social life and the Embassy children could run wild. Because there were so many children, Suma had its own little school taught by a very strict, old-fashioned English teacher. For the first time we learned about pounds, shillings and pence and she told us about life in England. It all sounded very dull to us but she was a good teacher, even if I did leave a hatching wasps' nest in her desk overnight. They were angry wasps by the morning and we had three days off school while she recovered.

While we were off school the parents of my small gang were searching the compound grounds for the keys to the summer residence. It was winter at the time and the building was empty—a temptation which proved too much for us. I broke in and encouraged the others to help me go berserk through the big rooms. Whatever was there we smashed and then, finding the keys still in the massive locked doors, we took them all out and buried them. But we could not remember where, and our parents were faced with the bill. It was generally agreed that this episode was mostly my fault. After that, mothers would telephone to ask if my sister could come to tea or for the weekend but not me because I was too wild. I did not much mind; their homes always seemed unreal to me. The order and peace made me anxious.

My mother *did* mind, of course. She was greatly upset on one occasion when she had finally managed to wangle an invitation to tea with one of the famous hundred families who controlled most of Persia. We all sat in a formal circle on the veranda of their beautiful summer house, in the middle of their tea gardens. The conversation was extremely stilted. I was sitting on an uncomfortable chair, holding a cup of tea, when I felt something crawling up my leg. It felt very large and very resolute. I looked down and there was probably the biggest spider I have ever seen in my life making its way up to my kneecap. I screamed and leapt straight up into the air. The cup smashed and I was sobbing with fright.

My mother was furious. How dare I behave in such a fashion as to embarrass her in front of the famous family? Obviously, to her, what other people felt about you was more important than what you felt about yourself. She constantly referred to 'other people'. Her life was a constant race to catch up, keep up with and impress them. I decided that about this time that I had had enough of those 'other people' who always knew best and for whom my feelings were continually being sacrificed, and I adopted a rude sullen pose. The more rich, famous or important the guest, the more obstreperous I became. But my sister went the other way and we remain like that.

While my mother was busy chatting up rich Persians, my father was at work in the city, and used to come back late. I spent most of my life in the compound running wild. The ground there was covered in 'shy grass' which was like clover but would shrink into a limp strand if you touched it. It tasted bitter and delicious. Everywhere there were carpets of hyacinths and you could lie on your back drunk with the smell. The houses were festooned with purple bougainvillaea, and in the evening the white faces of the morning glory suddenly opened in between the ropes of dark green ivy that hung off the trees.

Animals were much more fun than 'other people'. Lying at the bottom of a little cone of sand, awaiting any heavy-footed insect, was the Lion ant. I could spend hours on my stomach watching the flurry and the struggle. Usually I would rescue the victim or head it off, and then tickle the ant. The Lion ant would heave and strain, clutching at my straw, and I would roll about laughing. I had my cat, a flea-infested hedgehog, and a mother dog that I found in a drain: she had nine puppies. There was a large communal swimming pool where I could always meet friends and swim. The swim had a good chance of being enlivened by a small bear that lived with the man up the road. The bear would join us in the pool, until one day it got bored with being sweet and furry and dug its claws deep into a child's leg. Poor bear was in disgrace and was shipped home to the Zoo in Regent's Park. Years later I wandered round the terraces and there he was sitting mournfully on his haunches swaying. We looked at each other trapped in a grey English winter's day—I remembered him as a small, round, fat, happy bear in a hot country and I wondered if he remembered me as a furious skinny tom-boy who could swim as fast as he could.

I broke my wrist in Persia when I was roller-skating with friends down the rough road that led to the swimming pool. I fell and my feet flew up into the air. I put out my hand to save myself, leaned heavily on it and felt a terrible pain in my wrist. I looked down to see my hand hanging limply off my wrist. I sent my companion to my mother to tell her my arm was broken. She sent back a message to say there was nothing wrong with my legs and I was to walk home. During the hours of waiting that followed, while a car was found to take me to hospital, I was not allowed to cry or complain. Having been ignored as a child, my mother coped with illness and pain without complaining and she expected us to do the same. Later she found a particular butcher of a dentist to deal with my terrible teeth and she would sit while he drilled huge holes in my agonized jaws—no anaesthetic and no tears: "Noblesse oblige," she would say.

The summer before we left Persia we went with some other families into the mountains to escape the worst of the heat. The Persian mountains were famous for their views and the most beautiful spot was the Lar Valley. Here the Shah of Persia bred his beautiful Arab horses. We started the journey by car with two lorries piled high with equipment: it was the custom to spend two weeks packing for a stay of eight weeks. Once we arrived in the foothills the lorries and cars disgorged their occupants and the tents, cooking equipment and bedding were transferred on to the backs of a train of mules. The families got on to the horses and the smaller children, like my brother, rode on the pommel of the saddle in front of an adult. The cavalcade set off up the mountains with the cries of the muleteers echoing back down the train as they urged the animals on.

We travelled all day and most of the night. The roads became narrower and steeper until the horses seemed to be climbing almost vertically, scrambling with their hooves and the stones rattling down behind them. The path was lit by servants carrying poles with hissing paraffin lamps which cast a yellow-green light over the procession. We stopped only if a mattress slipped off or if we needed to break for a meal. Finally we arrived in the early grey misted dawn. The valley where we were to camp lay in the crutch of two long ranges of mountains. The business of setting up camp began in earnest as soon as the families dismounted. The army of servants that accompanied us began to unload and set up the huge tents, as big as circus tents. Ours had a central sitting room, a dining room, and round the outside corridor there were four bedrooms. Quite the largest, hairiest spiders I have ever seen could be seen starting up the walls. More tents were set up as kitchens and lavatories.

The American families who camped nearby drove the English

families mad because, for a start, they were 'oil' families with much more money and their equipment was far superior to ours. But the main struggle was over hygiene, as the Americans sterilized everything and if they could not boil it they dropped pills in it. This was much to the disgust of the English who have believed since time immemorial that germs, like natives, will not attack the English. We were proved right and the American families had dysentery almost all the time they were there.

During the day the children wandered freely in spite of the dangers, among them a large quicksand that would be lethal should anyone fall in. I spent many happy hours feeding long sticks into the quaking shifting sands. It was fun to wrestle with each other on the edge of the pool, pushing almost but not quite hard enough to risk falling in. My little brother was found trying to climb up the back leg of a mule and to my disgust the mule refused to kick his head in. I was still furiously jealous of my brother because my mother adored him. With the setting of the sun we would all straggle home towards the camp and the adults. The tables outside the tents would be laid with white linen and silver, and the cooks would serve huge meals beaming with pride. After dinner the adults would play cards, talk or read and we would sit just out of range of the lamplight watching the fireflies and the little jumping jerboas which looked like a cross between a rat and a kangaroo. Then we would be sent to bed, and as I curled down to sleep I heard the hyenas giggling and the jackals howling at the moon.

Just before the end of the holiday my mother told us that we would be going back to England, where my sister and I would probably go to boarding school. England conjured up visions of well-ordered living. It was the sound of Big Ben at six o'clock in the evening and a faint prune voice reciting cricket scores, tissue-thin newspapers, parcels from Fortnums, Harrods, the Army & Navy, and stories of other children about proper schools and Cash's name tapes. I didn't like the sound of England at all.

Once back in the compound, out came the familiar wooden crates. On the day we were due to leave our house my cat brought out her kittens which she had hidden in the attic away from my over-friendly attentions. She knew I was going and she threaded through my legs one last time. I said goodbye to my menagerie and my sister and I jammed in the car incoherent with grief. We waved goodbye to the cook and the maidservant, who were to be bequeathed to the next family. The Embassy guards clicked their heels as we drove through the gates for the last time and it seemed the end of freedom for a long while.

FOUR

England: School and St Mary's

ON THE DOCK we sailed from, a permanent party for those arriving and departing had seemed to be going on. Vendors barged through the crowd selling sticky cakes and lurid ice-creams from trays round their necks. Cows wandered perilously near the edge of the road and cars screamed up beside the ship to disgorge still more ebullient men and women bent on saying lingering and noisy good-byes. At the English end, however, it was dreadfully quiet. Amidst the organized efficiency of the docks, knots of silent, unsmiling people stood about, supposedly waiting to welcome their families back from the East. When they met them they showed no emotion except for a squeeze of the shoulder or a nervous wave of the hand. I was used to huge milling groups of people hugging and kissing each other, all wearing flowing robes of every conceivable hue. Here I looked in vain for a flash of colour or a warm brown face. In England, I noticed, white men carried your suitcases. I had never seen that before.

Most of all I missed the smell of the East, of incense mixed with a corrupt smell of garbage and cow dung, suffused with the heavy scent of the frangipani trees, whose flowers symbolize death. If you stand by the trees in the evening you can become besotted by the perfume wafting from the heavy waxen blooms. The smell of England was of soot and mean streets, a slightly sour smell. I was so homesick for the frangipani trees I cried as the train from Southampton sniffed past cramped houses, huddled together in rows behind grimy lace curtains.

My mother, in common with many other colonials, had a totally unrealistic view of life in England. She should have realized after her first disastrous honeymoon trip round the world, which had included a visit to my father's relations, that, contrary to her expectations, she had not married into the English upper classes. However, she was very good at forgetting the past, and blithely chose to rent a place in the country, in Devon, even though there was no question of my father being accepted by the local landed gentry.

After six months in England my parents were to go to China for a two-year posting. My father was very pleased about this, as he loved China. When he had first been sent there, as a very young man, he had spent years in strange-sounding places up extraordinary rivers, learning Chinese and living in Chinese families. If he belonged anywhere in the world, it was probably China, so now, in England, he was in a much more relaxed mood than usual.

The first sight of our house in Devon did little to reassure me about England. It was a bungalow, very cramped and confined compared to the houses with big open rooms and wide verandas we had left behind. It was crammed full of furniture, while the houses we were used to had been very sparsely furnished because in the heat empty rooms tended to feel cooler. Of course I felt disillusioned, being too young to realize that the life lived abroad by upholders of the British Empire was ridiculously extravagant, and that the British at home had just been through a World War. When I marched into the local sweet shop to buy five shillings' worth of sweets, I discovered first of all that the lady was not prepared to be beaten down to four shillings and sixpence (indeed she became very hostile when I tried it), and secondly, that she would not part with the sweets at any price when she found I did not have a ration book.

These were hard lessons to learn, but we slowly settled. I tried to make friends with the local children who said 'Go away, pig face', which hurt. Then my mother got to know a very nice woman who had a daughter the same age as my sister and me and who owned three ponies. We were allowed to visit the family and to ride the ponies.

The father was always at home, as he did not work, and was very aggressive. He also made a point of touching me as I passed him. I remember sitting on the grass in their back garden and, as he walked by me, I saw his hot brown eyes flicker over me. Memories of the comic-seller came back to me, and I immediately asked him for money to buy sweets. He gave me some. We looked at each other. Like my father, he could be very easily manipulated.

Years later, in the refuge, a woman journalist said to me, 'I've just been to the play group. Your little girls are so friendly. They climbed all over me.' The remark struck a chord and I began to watch the girls very closely. The boys on the whole actively demanded attention; the girls got their way by flattery and seduction, just as I did all those years ago. And these are girls who are likely to end up as rape victims and prostitutes, because they have no mechanism warning them that a man may be dangerous, seeing him only as fair game for manipulation. It did not surprise me a few months ago to hear from the local police that my little girls from the play group were collecting pennies from men outside the lavatories. 'We just asked,' they said, when questioned, but behind their innocent stare lay a wealth of experience.

One day in Devon we were allowed to take the ponies out by ourselves. It was then, riding over the moors and through the fields, that I began to see that England offered a gentler and calmer way of life. There were definite seasons which followed one another punctually and unfolded without hurricanes, tornadoes or tremendous tropical downpours of rain. The Devon people were warm and kindly. We got to know the local farmer, to whom we went for our milk and eggs, and would play with his goats. I was amazed at his healthy growing animals. I watched the cows coming home, ambling gently up the road with the cowman strolling behind them. How different they were from the animals we had seen abroad, being chased and screamed at by their owners. In England there were no beggars in the street, no cringing dogs hunting for scraps or skeletal cats. It was all very peaceful. The main reason for my parents' return to England had been, as we knew, to put my sister and me into boarding school. My mother of course had had grand ideas of sending us to one of the famous public schools, but even she had to face the fact that neither of us would be able to pass even the simplest of entrance exams. Eventually, however, she heard about a convent school, to which we were to be sent as boarders for one term, to settle in before being left on our own in a strange country for two years. The nuns belonged to a very small French teaching order with one other house in England.

The junior school was not very prepossessing, but the nun who ran it was a marvellous, dynamic little Irishwoman, who had a silver tongue with razor-sharp edges. My first memory of the school was of nun-green walls and long, long polished corridors, along which children walked slowly and in silence. The uniform was a navy-blue tunic, white blouse and striped tie. Underneath you wore a Clydella vest and a pair of white knickers, over which you pulled on a pair of navy-blue bloomers—changed once a week. I was lucky because my sister and I were in the same dormitory, and the nun who ran it was a young and gentle girl. I think she really grieved for the children, who were aged five upwards. She would always tuck us up and if you had been sobbing, as many of us had, she would sometimes give you a kiss, which was very comforting. I was quite happy there.

On our floor lived a very old, gnarled woman. I thought that she must be at least a hundred years old. It was the nuns' job to care for her as well. The old lady had been very rich and she was to leave all her money to the school, provided she was looked after until she died. Sometimes she would stagger out of her room dressed in a long white gown, her hair in grey hanks over her shoulder, and her eyes milk-white. 'Sister, Sister!' she would screech, and we learned to guide her back to bed and then find Sister. Sometimes she would be near death, and the priest would go past our room carrying the monstrance, which was made of gold, shaped like the sun, with sparkling rays and with the host in the centre, encased in glass. Beside the priest flapped the nuns with their long dark robes, and behind them, ringing the bell, came the server with his white lace sleeves. The procession passed into the room to administer the last rites to the dying woman, and when they left, to travel back along the black corridors, the sound of the bell would lie shivering in the silence. Then one night I heard busy scuffling after they left, and the next morning when I looked into the old lady's room through the door that had been left open, the bed was stripped and empty—she had died.

For the first time, I became aware of organized religion. So far, I had been aware of God, or, perhaps, the worship of different sorts of gods in other countries. The call to prayer which I had heard in Beirut and in Teheran sounded every day. The chants of the priests came nasal and high-pitched across the cities, and grown men put rugs on the ground and knelt to say their prayers. In our family, very little attention was paid to religion, except for the prayers we had been taught as children, which went, 'God bless Mummy and Daddy, and make Mei-Mei and Chei-Chei good girls'. Now I was exposed to the full ritual of the Catholic Church. Though we were not Catholic we were expected to attend the services which, with the ever-present light and the tabernacle that housed a real and living Presence, assumed enormous proportions in my mind. The catechism we learnt by heart and the lessons that taught us the almost permanent state of sin in which our innocent childish souls existed, made me acutely aware of my immoral and anti-social behaviour. It did little to change me, but it overlaid my feelings with an anxious sense of doom-laden hellfire, so that I would pray frantically for forgiveness before going back into school life, to sin again. Loud laughter, running in the corridor, eating more than your fair share, immoral thoughts, getting out of bed late: the list of my transgressions was endless.

In our dormitory, the rule was that you filled your jug with hot water every morning and evening, and you drew your curtains across the little cubicle where you slept, and washed and dressed in secret. I slept next to the nun and found a hole in the wood through which I watched her undressing. In fact, I only wanted to see if she really had a bald head under her wimple, but my intentions were misunderstood when I was discovered, and I was considered to have committed a deeply mortal sin. I was sent alone to the chapel, where I was left late into the night to contemplate my sins. It was dark and a candle flame flickered in a red glass over the coffin of one of our gentle nuns who had died. I was hungry and tired, and frightened; by the time a nun, the piano teacher for the school, rescued me, I was sobbing and shaken. She took me into her little camphor-smelling room, where she kept the medicines to cure coughs and colds, gave me a handful of sugar-coated cough pills and sent me, much comforted, to bed.

As a pupil I was generally considered stupid and slow. My writing and spelling made anything I tried to do hopeless, and I was punished again and again for being careless and lazy. I was given endless lists of words to learn by heart, but I would know them for five minutes, and then they would be gone. It was the school inspector who eventually recognized that I had some potential. One day when he came into our classroom, he decided to tell us stories of the Norse gods. I knew them all, and helped him out. He switched to stories of the Greek Gods. I knew them too. He tried poetry. I knew longer and better poems than he did. He gave up and told the Mother Superior that I would go far. But my store of knowledge seemed irrelevant to the English educational system, and I sat through hours of lessons, slowly losing interest in learning anything at all. It showed at the end-of-term results, where I was nearly always at the bottom of the class. For the rest of my school career, I remained there. It seemed to me that any effort I made in the classroom could only bring failure and disappointment, so I opted out of education and gave up. But my mother begged the nuns to keep us anyway, when she and my father went to China, and they agreed. They knew by then that I was going to be a difficult child.

When the time came for my parents to leave for China, they kissed us goodbye in the school drive. It was dark and my brother, who was going with them, was crying. We dimly realized that we would not see them again for a long time. My father was crying. He cried very easily. I do not remember my mother showing any emotion at all. As they drew away in the car my sister tried to hold on to the door, but I pulled her away, knowing it would do no good at all. We were alone, and we were to remain alone for three years: no sooner had my parents arrived in Tientsin than the Communist take-over of China began, and they were put under house arrest.

We were puzzled that for a long time no letters came from China. Eventually we gathered what had happened, and first heard the mysterious words 'house arrest'. One day the Latin teacher, who was standing outside the school, waiting for a lift into town, turned to me as I was passing and remarked that it was a tragedy that we might possibly never see our parents again. I reported this remark to my sister and we both considered it carefully. Our relationship with them had never been particularly close, so we could feel no real grief. We both tended to think of our mother as a very beautiful and fragile doll, and as our main anxiety was that she should not be hurt, we went on writing our weekly letters about nothing in particular, and were careful never to give her any cause for worry. Even if we had written about our unhappiness at school, it would probably not have got through, as Mother Madeleine had all the letters read.

By then we had moved to the senior school, which was in a very beautiful Georgian manor house. It stood in carefully wooded grounds which had a graceful Italian belvedere with a well and semi-circular seats overlooking rolling fields of wheat. The entrance to the building had the usual sweeping drive and the entrance hall, paved with marble, led into a small drawing room where the Reverend Mother interviewed the new pupils. Before we were taken before her we were taught to curtsy. Then, in the drawing room with its ornate Italian frescoes, I sat with my feet neatly together, remembering that a lady never crossed her legs.

The Reverend Mother would tell each new child of her hopes for their future, and that the greatest ambition for a girl at our school was that she would be presented to the Queen and then marry well. Girls who passed exams and got a place at University were honoured by the school having an afternoon off in celebration. This was such a rare event that there was no danger of it happening oftener than once or twice a year. On such occasions, whilst munching our way through the extra food provided, we all felt a little sorry for the girl, because going to University was, in fact, admitting that she had little potential and would have to earn her own living.

Although the Reverend Mother was the official head of the school, it was actually Mother Madeleine, the Mother Superior, who ran things. I hated her at first sight. She had a tiny round face and a thin mean line for a mouth. Her eyes behind her glasses were cold blue marbles and she was ruthless. The story was that she had been the brilliant child of a very poor family. Her education had been financed by the religious order and the price she had had to pay was to become a 'bride of Christ'. Certainly I never detected in her anything remotely approaching the love and compassion traditionally expected of someone in the service of God. On the contrary, she behaved exactly like the ambitious managing director of a large building firm—except that, instead of bricks and mortar, she had power over hundreds of vulnerable children, and some of us paid a terrible price.

My sister and I were not equipped to live in close quarters with regimented middle-class children. The values and intricacies of the English class system were very strange to us, and the routine we had begun to find intolerable at the junior school was even more inflexible now. My sister conformed, became covered in weeping eczema, and was always ill. I rebelled, broke the rules, and was always in trouble. And now, in the senior school, I was no longer one of the biggest bullies in the school, but rather a small bully in a large pool of girls up to the age of eighteen.

A deviant, delinquent child was like a red rag to a bull where Mother Madeleine was concerned. She set out with all the power that she had to force me to conform to the standards she had dictated for the school. No talking in corridors. I sang loudly. She punished me. No breaking school bounds. I roamed all over the forbidden woods. She punished me. No climbing on the roof. I was up there, perilously hanging from the gutters. She punished me. They separated me from my sister, presumably believing she would be better off away from my boisterous, over-dominating presence. She probably was, but I was desolate because I had such terrible nightmares. I had had a habit of leaving my bed in the middle of the night and getting into hers, where she would comfort me. Now she was long corridors away, and I would creep up and down them in the dark, in an effort to get to her. But the nuns would turn me back. Then I would lie rigid with fear, with the pillow over my face, hoping that whoever my unknown assailant was, he would pass my bed, believing it to be empty.

I had little free time because the punishments extended to detention, which meant spending hours in the library after class, and during weekends. My meals were taken outside the dining-room door, seated at a table by myself. After I ate, I would have to help the sisters who were the school servants to wash up. I never minded, because they were so kind and friendly to me. The room piled high with plates and cups would be full of steam from the taps which vomited streams of boiling water into the big sinks, where the sisters laboured with their long sleeves pinned back, their arms bare to the elbow. They laughed and joked as they worked. Then the bell would ring, and I would have to go back to the classroom to behave badly until I was sent outside. Being an outsider became almost comfortable. It was a way of life.

All the younger girls had 'pashes'. Each would single out an older girl as an object of affection, and pursue her with letters, notes under her pillow and presents. The little girls needed their 'pashes', to giggle and suffer over, but they were also encouraged by the older girls as a mark of popularity. In fact, these relationships had very little to do with sex; if you take young girls away from home at an early age, naturally they will look for love and affection to replace what they have been deprived of. The nuns never touched or kissed any of us, and it was a very bleak, emotionally impoverished experience to spend twelve or thirteen weeks in a place without anyone to tuck you up and kiss you goodnight. No wonder that the little girls vied for the affection of the older, mother-substitute figures. I immediately found a girl, who not surprisingly looked like my mother, but because I was unable to show any sort of affection, my aggressiveness puzzled her considerably. If she had to supervise the library, I would force her to send me out. If she captained a team of netball players, I played so badly she would have to lecture me on loyalty.

Nothing anyone could have done to me in that school could have altered my behaviour. My father was the dominant force in my life, the only person I would obey. Other adults irritated me like gnats, and I was able to ignore them. The matron was the only person at the school who had the remotest idea of how to cope with me. She was a practical middle-aged woman who looked after the domestic and medical affairs of the place and ran the infirmary, where I wanted to spend the rest of my life. But, apart from dreadful sore throats, I was very rarely ill, and however bad my throat the rule was that you had to have a temperature to be officially ill. I tried everything: taking off my socks and standing in puddles in bitter weather; eating poison berries and roots and anything I could bear to force down my throat in the garden. On the few occasions I got admitted to the infirmary it was bliss and I was happy. Matron would fuss over and care for me. She let me read far into the night and listen to Radio Luxemburg and the Top Twenty. Best of all, she would come in and straighten out the bed last thing at night and kiss me. These were very warm and happy moments. Then I would be decanted into the school again, and Mother Madeleine would be there, her face white with fury over some further outrage.

Matron could often be seen dashing down the corridor, carrying a bowl with a towel draped over it. Underneath it would be a packet of sanitary towels, and she was on her way to a dormitory to slip the packet discreetly into a cupboard. A girl's periods or the 'curse' were never discussed, even though the class I was in was fascinated by the subject, whispering about it together in tight knots whenever the chance came. We would go into the lavatories and count the used sanitary towels in the bins, then lurk outside until a more senior girl had gone in, and when she left the lavatory go in and count again. I was desperate to be the first in the class to own a mysterious packet and to be acknowledged as a woman before anyone else.

I got so impatient at waiting I told Matron that I had started and she believed me. I had a marvellous time demanding days off Mass because of severe abdominal cramps. Lying palely on my bed, racked with pain, I could see the respect I commanded from the rest of the dormitory. However, I overdid it as usual, and three packets of sanitary towels later, Matron asked me to take down my knickers, and there, between my legs, lay the snow-white towel. Disgrace! Mother Madeleine was told. She did not understand. She was angry. How could she ever understand the significance of a first period for a girl? However much you know it means discomfort, sanitary towels and blood, it is also the first step towards joining the world of women. But for me it was just another milestone that should have been a happy and healthy experience, but which was twisted and distorted for me.

By the time my periods did arrive, I had long stopped worrying about them; I was much more concerned about the fact that I was developing a large bosom and did not have a bra. Lots of the girls wore bras, but my mother was now back in contact with us, and as her instructions were that young girls should never wear any form of support, because the muscles would waste away, there was little I could do about it. So I hunched my shoulders and wore my school blazer all the time. I sweated in the heat but I would not remove it. I could not bear the undisciplined bulges that wobbled about every time I moved. Finally, Matron took pity on me, and bought me and my sister some horrific-looking contraptions sold off cheaply by the Air Force. But I was glad of them. At last, I could take my blazer off.

Though we were getting to be women, some sooner than others, the subject of procreation was not supposed to be discussed. The whole area of sex education was left to the science teacher, whose main contribution was a lecture on pollination, followed by a very sketchy outline of the behaviour of rabbits, and then an announcement that it was exactly the same for human beings. She had a broad Scots accent, and spat furiously when she became excited. By the time she had progressed from pollination to rabbits, she was beside herself and had drenched the first two rows. The vital information, thus mangled by her accent and confused by saliva, failed to instruct us during our most formative years. It was much more essential for me than for the others, because I had no one to whom I could turn, and though I fumbled frantically through books in the library, they were all so well censored that there was no reference at all to the physical facts. We were allowed pets, and I had a rabbit with the original name of 'Lady'. In deadly secret I let her loose with the school rabbit called Peter. The resulting union produced not only further rabbits but—at last—enlightenment.

However, at that age my sexual curiosity was insatiable, and I found a few other girls with a store of dirty jokes and filthy rhymes which we would swap and elaborate and generally enjoy the sensation of lewd pleasure in repeating them. These were 'day girls', much looked down upon, who were mostly the daughters of the aspiring Catholic middle classes in the town. They were despised because it was assumed that their parents could not afford boarding fees. Besides, they were 'common', and they had West Country accents. I found them to be very much like myself, and even though day girls rarely mixed with boarders, I spent my free time in their company.

One day one of them, Sylvia, came to school in a terrible state saying that she had been raped by her father. We were in the cloakroom at break—just a knot of sympathizers. Her dad had been drunk, and she had been lying on the sofa in the sitting room at home when he came back. He had got on top of her and begun heaving up and down. We all cried in sympathy, and a prefect came in and flushed us out into the garden. I was the last to leave because I was practising a bow-legged walk which I imagined one would have to adopt after such a disastrous incident, and the tears of self-pity blinded me. The prefect, alarmed at this scene, asked me kindly if I was all right. The gentle tone of her voice was too much, and I threw myself into her arms and, having first sworn her to secrecy, I told her the whole tragic story. She reacted with such shock and horror that I was instantly gratified and considered my future in the theatre. I left the cloakroom, assured of her silence, and went to find my friends.

That night we were all herded into Assembly and the Reverend Mother gave us a very long lecture on how it was forbidden to discuss anything that might sully the shining purity of our souls. I did not listen very much because I knew my soul was such a muddy morass of slime and sin. It went on for a very long time. After we were dismissed I went off to bed, ready to dig out my torch and my copy of *Gone With the Wind* to read under the covers. I should have suspected that something was wrong when Mother Madeleine came in to put out the lights. Sex seemed to inspire a lot of snooping on her part. Her face had a disgusted, white, pinched look—the face she usually assumed when dealing with me—but she said nothing at all.

She said the usual prayer that night: 'Into Thy hands, O Lord, I commend my spirit.' Once having said that you were officially in a state of grace, and should you be taken short and die in the night, you would be exempt from seven hundred light-years of Purgatory. The more religious girls in the school advocated lying flat, with hands crossed on the breast, so that, in the event of death, the whole thing would be dignified. This nightly contemplation of the possibility of death, at the age of twelve and thirteen, was a strain, but we muttered the prayer every night and prepared for the inevitable. And, should we escape the awful moment, we knew that at 6.45 next morning, those of us who had survived would hear Mother Madeleine say, 'Praise be to Jesus Christ', and on the 'Amen' your feet were supposed to hit the floor, before you crashed to your knees with fervent thanks for having got through the night. It was touch-and-go all the time.

The next morning the class was called into the drawing room.

Sylvia, we were told, would not return to the school. She had been found guilty of telling wicked lies about her father. Her mother and father had been called to the school, and she had been confronted by Mother Madeleine before their arrival. The parents were told that she could not be allowed to stay and she was expelled on the spot. I sat absolutely still while mice scrabbled frantically in my brain and cold fingers closed around my heart. 'Of course,' said Mother Madeleine, 'Sylvia knew exactly who to go to with her sordid little story.' She beckoned me to follow her into the office. I got up and, feeling like an elephant, lumbered after her, all eyes in the classroom following me.

I was the only boarder involved in that particular scandal. I knew that Sylvia was not lying. I had been badly frightened at times in my life, and I had been able to sense the fear in that girl. I also realized that it was Mother Madeleine's instinct to protect the school against scandal and that the individual counted for very little in her world. I listened to the usual harangue. The usual threats were issued, but I knew that we were stuck with each other. She had nowhere to expel me to. 'You were born to be hanged,' she said. I knew she was probably right, and I wondered what had happened to Sylvia.

Bottom of the class, always in trouble, and not much liked by any of the adults, my life at the convent school was only made bearable by the holiday home in Devon, St Mary's, to which my sister and I were sent at Christmas and Easter, and in the summer vacation. In those days there were no provisions for flying children out to spend holidays with their parents, and there were usually about forty boys and girls, aged from six to eighteen, in the holiday home. Most of them were the children of parents posted abroad, who, like ours, had wanted them to attend good English public schools, and who had no close relations to whom they could send them for holidays, so had been forced to leave them in the care of virtual strangers. We were lucky to have been sent to St Mary's, which was run in a way that was a complete contrast to the rigid formality of the convent school and provided a warm, kindly base for us.

St Mary's was a mock-Tudor Victorian pile surrounded by 250 acres of woods and forests, owned and run by a woman called Miss

Williams. She was in her fifties when I first went there, and I always remember my first sight of this enormous woman. She was about six feet four inches tall, and must have weighed at least twenty stone. She bent down and looked at me with such kindness in her very blue eyes that I immediately felt safe in her presence. Not even my father, I felt, would tangle with anyone her size. Probably one reason why I remain deliberately overweight now, in spite of my doctor's warnings, is that I realize how much comfort my size gives women and children. And there is nothing more terrifying for a man than a very large and determined woman; often when I stand on the doorstep of the refuge, facing a very disturbed and distressed husband, I feel him at first react fearfully, expecting me to be angry with him, and then relax and usually break down. As I explain that I do not approve of what he did, but that I still love him, I can tell that by being outsize, I fit his vision of the loving mother he never had. My size also gives me a lot of confidence when I have to deal with officials who disapprove of Chiswick Women's Aid. The larger you are the harder it is for blank-faced civil servants to disregard your presence.

At St Mary's the house was a warren of rooms, with an extension built on to house the older boys. The upstairs was divided up into dormitories named after the rivers of Devon. These were extremely spartan, with iron beds and small lockers for our few personal possessions. The younger children slept in the main body of the house, and the older children were in dormitories next to and below Miss Williams's room, where she could keep a motherly eye on them. My own dormitory was directly underneath her room with an open shaft that led into her room. She could hear if we talked late at night, and her ghostly, authoritative voice would float down the shaft at intervals if we made too much noise.

Miss Williams was an old-fashioned Christian. She lived her life, sure in her belief in God, and in the essential goodness of every human being. We went to church every Sunday in our best clothes, and were not allowed to smoke or swear; nor were we allowed to drink, except for a glass of cider on Christmas Day. In spite of the huge range in our ages, and the undoubted problems many of us had, she was respected by us all, and if one of us was found guilty of bad behaviour, the surprised hurt in her face was quite enough to keep us under control. She had a few ingenious punishments which she used when we pushed her too far. The most diabolical was making us peel hundreds of globe artichokes, under the supervision of the kitchen staff. I must have peeled acres of artichokes in my time, and I still cannot face eating them without feeling a twinge in my fingers.

Many of the children at St Mary's were disturbed and often quite violent, and the house was a wasteland of battered and scarred furniture, as few objects survived our unruly onslaughts. Because most of us had never lived in our own homes, but rather in company houses or ones belonging to the Foreign Office, we had little respect for property. Miss Williams made no attempt to police the house, but let us value the few things we really used, like the ping-pong table and the old wind-up gramophone; when they got broken, she did not offer to have them mended until we clubbed together to pay for it with our pocket money. In the new wing, which was built shortly after my arrival at St Mary's, a huge room was set aside for the older boys' model-making. The boys spent most of their holidays building complicated aircraft, some with petrol engines, and the more expert made remote-control planes. Much of our time was spent up on the moors watching them fly, the younger children acting as retrievers and scaling trees to rescue planes that refused to return to their owners.

There was no television at St Mary's, and we were only occasionally allowed to go to the local cinema, accompanied by Miss Williams. When she decided that there was a film worth seeing, we were packed like sardines into an old estate car, and disgorged outside the cinema, where the manager would receive her like royalty. We were shown up to the front circle and sat in a long row. When we were with Miss Williams we all behaved beautifully, and we watched the film hoping that we would be allowed to see the supporting feature. However, we were very rarely so lucky; usually, after a quarter of an hour of the second film, Miss Williams would snort loudly, and announce in ringing tones that it was highly unsuitable for children. Heaving herself out of her chair, she would set off for the exit, followed by a long file of highly embarrassed children. I do not think I ever saw a whole programme in all the time I was at St Mary's.

Most of our entertainment we had to make for ourselves. During the day, the smaller children played camps and houses in the thick woods and dense rhododendrons, and the older ones played card games and chess. Evenings we spent in the playroom with the old wind-up gramophone, dancing the two-step, Scottish reels and the Moonlight Saunter.

Because there were very few adults to run the home, the children naturally formed their own pecking order. The older girls mothered the little ones, and the older boys worked with 'Fursey', who lived in the cottage, as he chopped logs and heaved coal; also, generally under a certain amount of duress, they dug in the vegetable garden which provided the fresh food for the kitchen. The children who returned year after year formed a nucleus of group opinion, which controlled the behaviour of the community. It was, for instance, permissible to go for long walks with a boy you considered attractive. However, you were also aware that you were being followed closely by small children, who would report back to the house any piece of spicy information for everyone else to savour and enjoy. Indeed, anything more than a chaste kiss was considered 'fast', and a girl risked being ostracized by the other girls for loose behaviour.

I had my first real boyfriend at St Mary's. After a New Year's party, Michael and I had managed to Moonlight Saunter right out of the back door, and he kissed me on the mouth. Just as I was making a mental note on the situation, we were disturbed by an outraged roar from Miss Williams, who was behind a bush where she had been waiting for one of her dogs to pee. 'How disgusting!' she yelled at the top of her considerable voice. 'Just like film stars!' and she seized both of us by the scruff of the neck and hauled us back into the playroom, where the others were standing in horrified silence. There, she delivered a long lecture on respect and chaps who did not respect a gel, and gels who made themselves cheap. I felt very cheap indeed and slunk off to bed.

It did not stop us trying again, but Michael had been seeing too many films, and thrust his tongue down my throat, which made me go purple in the face, and put me off kissing for a very long while. I much preferred James, who was very big and silent. In fact, he was so silent that we would walk for miles without a word being said, and the only gauge of his emotional state would be the sweat pouring off his brow and the clammy grip of his mighty hand on mine. It was very satisfying, especially at mealtimes, when one smouldering glance across the porridge would send him deep purple, and a vein would throb in his neck.

I do not remember ever being bored at St. Mary's because each holiday contained and was based on a festivity. Christmas, for example, began on the day we arrived. In the hectic first days of the holiday Miss Williams would be whizzing up and down to Axminster station, collecting children, suitcases and tuck boxes. All the old faces appeared, looking apprehensive and amazed at the noise and chaos, but settling in rapidly after a few minutes' hesitation. Then the preparations began. Each dormitory was given the responsibility of a room to decorate and an entertainment to provide for the party. This would take hours of planning, after which all the decorations had to be made and the costumes for the party. The huge Christmas tree was put in its traditional place in the hall and the sacks of presents arriving for the children were piled up in the attic under lock and key.

By Christmas Eve excitement ran like an electric current through the house. The little ones were in bed early with one of Miss Williams's lisle stockings draped over the end of each bed, and the older ones taken to the local church for midnight service. The Christmas Eve church service was very important to Miss Williams, and, as we followed her into the little church, we were aware of her great faith, and tried not to fidget or contemplate our empty stomachs, while we joined in the carols and listened to the lengthy sermon. When it was over, we stumbled out into the night, surging up the narrow path policed by tombstones, wishing everyone a happy Christmas. The stars always seemed particularly brilliant that night, and the peace and hope of a good year ahead stayed with me for days.

When we arrived back at the house, we all stood round the fire, drinking mugs of cocoa and eating huge chunks of buttered bread. Then we slowly filed off into the darkened house on tiptoe, past the rooms of the already sleeping smaller children and into bed. Miss Williams would spend the early hours of the morning filling countless stockings with oranges, nuts, pencils and small toys, and we would wake to shrieks and yells of the younger boys and girls tear-ing open their presents and blowing loudly on tin whistles and trumpets.

Christmas Day unfolded according to tradition. After breakfast, we gathered under the tree for the first distribution of presents. The huge mail sacks were brought down and Miss Williams would hand out the presents to the children. It was a sad time for my sister and me, because our mother rarely bothered to send more than one parcel with a few ill-chosen items. As the other children gathered their ever-growing mountains of gifts around them, we waited hopefully, but as the distribution went on we knew that there would be nothing else for us and we would comfort each other. Many children received presents from relations and friends, as well as their parents, but we had none. Our awareness of a lack of concern on the part of our parents always spoiled Christmas Day for us, even though we joined in the huge party, the charades, the entertainments put on by each dormitory, and the dancing, and finally the singing as we went to bed on Christmas night.

The Easter holidays were less exciting, but on Easter Day there was an early morning church service followed by a huge Easter egg hunt which spread all over the grounds, and the hard-boiled eggs carefully dyed in all colours would be waiting for us afterwards, sitting upright and immaculate in their egg cups, when we came back to breakfast. Besides, spring had arrived and the forest was full of feathery green shrubs and bushes. We were able to run wild for miles up the bridle paths and hurtle over the moors in gangs, and to lie in the bracken eating our sandwiches and talking for hours about the business of the day and the future.

The summers were spent on the beach at Lyme Regis. The weather was immaterial. We were ferried by car to the Cob, where we established our base and spent the day swimming and exploring round the old harbour. The best swimmers swam from the harbour back to the pebbled beach, but although I could swim well, I hated the strands of seaweed that stroked my belly and the slimy feel of the bladderwrack as it scrunched under my bare scrabbling feet. Who knows what foul animal lurked under the stone, waiting to amputate a bare and defenceless toe or sink its teeth in my soft flesh as I passed by?

For all these happy times I shall always remember St Mary's.

When the holiday was over and it was time to return to school I would pack with a deep feeling of dread and unhappiness, and go to Miss Williams's sitting room to say goodnight as usual. One knocked on the door, and she would cry 'Come in'. Walking into the room was always a pleasurable shock. It was a long room with a big open log fire at the far end. All the winter months the grate was full of hissing, spitting logs, and the room smelt of pine and damp smoke. At that time of evening, Miss Williams would be sitting, as always, bolt upright in her winged armchair, her spectacles at the end of her nose, embroidering yet another chair seat. By the fire was a big dog-stained Chesterfield with two of the resident boxers—always bitches, and always on heat, hence the stains. The floor was highly polished with a few richly coloured rugs, and the standard lamps caught the gleaming lights from the big mahogany bookcases that lined the walls. It was always peaceful, and the large figure in the chair, the fire and the comfortable, civilized furniture gave me the hope that one day I would find a room or a place where I belonged. I would concentrate on the scene, and store it away for the troubled days at school, because I could always close my eyes and see it again when times were hard. Then I would kiss her goodnight and go to bed.

Sometimes we would go back to school by train, but often Miss Williams would drive us there herself. She hated Roman Catholics with a passion, and viewed the nuns with the deepest suspicion. They, in turn, felt that St Mary's was a den of vice and iniquity and a bad influence on us, and a cold hostility existed between the two parties. It must have been equally difficult for the other children at St Mary's to settle into the public schools chosen by their parents. Most public schools are merely extensions of the structure and expectations of middle-class family life. But none of us had ever experienced the social trials necessary to condition us to herd life. It was also true that most of us had dreadful school reports, and were backward in most lessons; though what we lacked in formal knowledge we made up for in independence and general information. At St Mary's, we were able to evolve a life that was comfortable and free from the petty irritations that would cause conflict.

That life reflected the unique blend of Miss Williams's powerful personality and her genuine innocence. She was an appalling businesswoman. She had an absolute passion for large estate cars and, in my time, she had at least six large Bedfords, which were more than she could afford, but she loved driving. She continually paid out far more money than she took in. She would never refuse to keep a child because the parents did not pay the fees. Indeed, many did not, and owed her money. But she always saw each child as an individual, and even the most belligerent boy was respectful in her presence.

My mother rarely made plans for us at half-term, and as the years went by, if we did not go to St Mary's we usually stayed at school. When the others had gone, my sister and I would roam the empty grounds and the classrooms. Occasionally some kind family would be asked by the nuns if they would have us to stay. My sister was always a popular guest. I was not. I hated staying in English houses; I found the rules too confusing. I never understood why people made such a fuss if you used their toothbrush instead of your own, or their towel, or why you had to sit at the table when you felt like leaving. Nor was I willing to try to learn. My sister was more diplomatic. I hated the families that kept horses in their stables covered in warm wool blankets, while I lay upstairs and froze under threadbare blankets. I hated the whole horsy, gymkhana, pony-club social life that claimed all the girls at the school.

Horses were basically there to embarrass me, by moving just as I was about to get on, or by kicking me just as I got off, or biting me if I took my eye off them for one minute. My sister had a natural seat, whatever that was, and as she cantered by the clumps of sheepskin coats huddled together perched on shooting sticks, all the heads would nod approvingly. But then I would shoot past holding on to the mane for dear life, and they would all suck their teeth, and shake their heads and I would feel their disapproval, as I vainly endeavoured to control the heaving, red-eyed beast and cursed them all into the wind and cursed their cold, pinched, pretentious houses.

These people's days were spent in the mud and slush doing things to their various horses. The most highly regarded pastime was the Hunt, when, like the Gadarene swine, they hurtled over high fences, risking life and limb to chase the fox which usually eluded them, but which occasionally died in a spray of blood and entrails, torn to pieces by the howling pack. I went along once, and was terrified at the lust which gripped both animals and humans. In the faces of many of the adults, as they watched the death throes of the fox, I saw a bestial pleasure in the cruel act, and I knew that they would have hunted a human being in the same way. They seemed to me to be the natural descendants of those who had sat in the arenas and watched men and women die. I never agreed to hunt again, but rather stayed in some chill house and waited for the others to come back.

At the end of the day's hunting, there was a pony-club dance. Usually held in some private house, these were dull affairs compared with the joyous dances at St Mary's. The pony-club children, who from an early age had been segregated in single-sex schools, had no idea of how to communicate with the opposite sex. The girls giggled dutifully and the boys thumped and bumped them around the room as so few of them had learned to dance. Contrary to Miss Williams's teaching, the 'fast gels' were very much in demand, and a shy, quiet girl would be almost totally ignored, unless she was from a very rich family, famous for good parties. The boys knew that they were all on lists, drawn up by the mothers, as eligible suitors for their daughters. How they behaved was immaterial. It was the size of inherited incomes and family estates that mattered. My sister and I were non-starters, and usually stood behind a potted palm, talked to aged relations of the family, or hung about the loo until it was time to go home. We both decided that English family life was not for us and began to refuse any invitations that came our way on the grounds that we had no clothes to wear.

In fact that was quite true. My mother had made no provision for clothing for us, apart from the usual uniform list with which we had been supplied when we first started the senior school. We soon grew out of the two non-uniform dresses we each owned, and finally Miss Williams was instructed to find second-hand clothes for us. We were both mortified. There was no disguising the fact that the garments were not only second-hand, that they were hopelessly old-fashioned. I was fat, which made it even more difficult for her to find anything for me, and when she did, it tended to be clothing for a much older woman, in which I looked and felt a freak.

I hated every moment I had to wear these clothes, especially at school, where it was unheard of for anyone to wear second-hand clothes. The girls soon sensed my humiliation and outrage, and Thursday evenings, when we had to change into 'mufti', were deeply embarrassing, as I struggled into the ill-fitting garments. I made up for the embarrassment by going berserk and picking fights, so that I was banished to the dormitory, where I could tear off the dress and get into bed and lose myself in a book.

When word at length filtered through that my mother was on her way back from the Far East, Mother Madeleine began to relax her grip on me. She left me alone during the weeks before my mother was due to arrive. She even smiled at me occasionally. And then one day she called me to the telephone. A strange voice said it was my mother, and that she had just arrived in England with my brother. I screamed back, 'You're not my mother. You don't speak like her. . . . You're fooling me.' I could not stop screaming and shaking. Mother Madeleine took the phone away from me and said soothing things to my mother and then put it down. I had been caught off-balance by the voice, because I had completely forgotten that my mother had a Canadian accent, and it sounded so strange to me. I ran upstairs to find my sister, who was in the bath at the time. She immediately submerged herself, crying hysterically, and we clung to each other. The nightmare of school would soon be over, we thought.

The next day, my mother arrived at the school. She had tea with the Reverend Mother and Mother Madeleine. I waited outside apprehensively. Would the nuns tell her how bad I had been? Would they tell her how they had had to punish me almost continually all the years she had been away? Would she hear about how I had let her down when she believed in me? They did not tell her. The three of them came out smiling and chatting gaily. Mother Madeleine was kind and gracious to me. I was so grateful that I could have kissed her. It was a pact.

Mother took us out to a huge tea, and my sister and I stuffed our faces and looked curiously at our brother, who seemed loud-mouthed and over-spirited. She gave us a pile of presents she had brought back with her for us, but they did not make up for the loss of the birthdays or Christmases that had gone unremembered. Then we returned to school to wait for the end of term. My mother was going to buy our first real home. A home of our own! And we were each going to have a room of our own.

Eventually she wrote to say that she had bought a house just outside Axminster, called 'Hunthay'. We arrived there in our school uniforms, clutching our suitcases, and gazed at this house which now belonged to our family. It seemed very small to us after St Mary's. It had four bedrooms, a thick thatched roof, a huge long drawing room, a square dining room-kitchen, a breakfast room, and outside there was a garden of one acre. It was not really small, but, to me, after the spaciousness of school and St Mary's, it was confining.

It was terribly quiet and we were dreadfully bored. For a start, my mother could not cook, and neither, of course, could we. Secondly, she was obsessively clean, but hated housework—as did we. Thirdly, she had grand ideas about the garden, but hated gardening—as did we. So she was stranded with two bored, rebellious, teenage daughters, who were not about to become her servants, as she had intended, and we found ourselves living with a woman whom we did not know very well, and who seemed to have one alarming scheme after another. She finally gave up her efforts at housework and employed a charlady, and as the weeds broke ranks in the garden she employed a gardener. However, neither accepted orders with the grace to which she was accustomed. At the slightest drop of rain, the gardener was inclined to crouch in the garage, mumbling over his pipe at people with foreign habits, while the char, an elderly middle-class woman who had fallen upon hard times, could scarcely be prevailed on to bend her knees as far as the floor.

We all managed to survive the holiday apart from a disastrous party organized by my mother for the St Mary's children. She could not understand that life at St Mary's was completely isolated and apart from home life. None of the children mixed the two in any way. The children who had been my close friends arrived, mute and clean, at the door. We looked at them and hoped they would understand parental pressures. We were all embarrassed for my mother, who had piled high the dining table with jellies, cakes and biscuits. She asked them to wash their hands. They would not, but watched us dutifully traipse to the bathroom and wash ours. We were captives, and they were so much freer. We lived in a neat house. We were living the family life we had yearned for for so many years, and now that we had it, we realized it was not family life we had been missing, but the loving that can really only come from one's own mother and father. Now we were old enough to comprehend that that was no longer a possibility for us.

The new house, the plans and dreams that my mother tried to share with us, were part of her own need to put right the humiliations and missed expectations of her own childhood. She was a princess who had never been made a queen. She spread out beautiful silks that she had brought back from China for us, material which was to make court dresses for a coming-out ball when we were eighteen. We looked at each other in despair. The St Mary's children listened with their heads on one side, and at last we were allowed to eat. I knew that my mother was disappointed. I think she had believed that since these children were from the best public schools in England, they would behave like the little heroes and heroines of old-fashioned novels. She did not realize that they mostly came from disturbed families and were the sons and daughters of fugitive parents.

My brother was put into prep school and returned home for weekends, white-faced and thin. The other boys had put his head down the lavatory and pulled the chain. They were paying him out for being different by tormenting and bullying him, and he was very little and helpless against it all. My mother was due to join my father in Dakar, in West Africa: a new posting and a new adventure. She was fed up with a servantless existence, and threw herself energetically into the new arrangements. My brother was to join us at St Mary's in the holidays. With all of us safely tucked up at school, she was soon ready to leave. The house was let and she delivered us back to the convent. Mother Madeleine waiting for me. It was the end of the truce.

FIVE

England: Lethal Games

LETTERS ARRIVED FROM West Africa, full of information about the exciting social life my mother was leading. We very rarely received a letter from my father, unless he was angry about our school reports which were always dreadful. It never crossed my parents' mind to question the school about its part in our poor reports. After all, we had been in the nuns' care for several years, and if we were consistently failing, perhaps the school was as much to blame as we were. My father's few letters were catalogues of his early sufferings and efforts to obtain an education, contrasting our luxurious lives with his threadbare existence, and bewailing the enormous sums of money it was costing him to keep us at the convent. To us it was a luxurious concentration camp, with Mother Madeleine gliding silently and malevolently round the perimeters, waiting for a chance to pounce.

When my mother left for Africa, we were fourteen, and I had begun to receive letters from the boys at St Mary's. All these were opened by Mother Madeleine and never passed on to me; but I would go down to her office late at night with a torch and read them for myself and then put them back. Ordinary people, I discovered, assumed that rules were made to be obeyed; but because I was outside the pale of normal behaviour, I could do largely as I pleased provided I was clever about it. The thought of entering Mother Madeleine's most sacred room was beyond the imagination of any girl at the school, so she never considered locking it.

Once I discovered the gullibility of most of the staff, I became quieter and everyone remarked upon my improvement. I had not improved at all, I had merely learned how to test each member of the staff, how to gauge their reactions and manipulate them accordingly. I may have failed almost all of my exams, but at the convent

Infernal Child

I did become a 'master' games player, which has stood me in good stead all my life. The best games players can usually be found in the criminal classes, and I tend to find myself most at home with a deviant group of women; in the refuge we talk about the games we all play. As most of our mothers have done the rounds of the agencies, and as expert games players have left a trail of prostrate social workers spread across various counties, it is quite comforting for them to come to a place where we accept their attempts at manipulating with good humour, but find them out fairly quickly.

Physical games, of course, were one of the most important parts of the school life. A lot of the hierarchy and power structure was based on one's ability to wield a hockey stick or pursue a wet ball furiously across muddy fields in driving rain. As I was a large, shambling girl, in hockey I was always chosen to play defence, and would spend hours thundering up and down the pitch, harassed by whistles; when the game ended, we would come to a juddering halt, scarlet in the face, panting and glowing, our legs purple and blotchy from the sleet. In the middle of one of my first hockey matches, the ball rose from the opponent's stick and hit me on the jaw. My teeth sank firmly into my bottom lip, and blood spurted on to my shirt. The referee wrenched open my jaw, and announced that it was not broken, slapped me firmly between my shoulder blades, and said that the game must go on. First I was to shake my opponent by the hand. 'No hard feelings,' she said, and I fought back a rising feeling of murderous rage, grasped the hand firmly and squeezed—to see the tears rising to her eyes. 'Of course not,' I said. The whistle went and the game went on.

Being in a team was the only way of getting away from school during term time, and one reason I had decided to play hockey was to enjoy the benefits of the exclusive teas that followed the matches. I joined the team in order to leave the school grounds in a coach, to visit other imprisoned girls like myself, and eat triumphantly in their dining rooms, exchanging gossip; also in order to look out of the windows during the journey and see ordinary people in the streets, doing very ordinary things, like shopping with their children, opening the doors of their little houses and walking through them with their children. I could imagine them all sitting down to tea, a real mother and father, with a teapot that was only for four or five, and a plate with a small cake on it that would be enough for everyone at the table. I had lived so long in institutions, where all the food came in large containers, and all eating was done in a furious atmosphere of competition, that I fantasized about a loving family life, and those journeys were necessary for me to check to see that the world outside still remained constant. We would sing on the way back from the matches and as we entered the school gates we would start to sing 'Land of Hope and Glory', our chests thrust out and voices quivering with emotion—except that for me the '. . . mother of the free' bit was overdoing it, considering we were entering a prison.

In summer we played cricket. I quite enjoyed the lazy days standing on the pitch in the hot hum of bees and insects, but I was afraid of the cricket ball that spun towards me, stinging my hands and making my fingers throb with pain. 'Oh, well done!' seemed to be the English way of congratulating you for enduring excrutiating pain. 'Oh, well done' meant you could not burst into tears, run off at high speed, or attack. As I was very good at catching the ball, I was moved in right up beside the batsman, to the most dangerous and therefore the most sought-after place in the team. I realized that I had been over-enthusiastic as usual.

Now it had been decided that I was to have the dubious honour of risking my life on the cricket field for the sake of the school, I was much fêted. During the week before the matches, we had a trial match against the B side, and they put one of our best batsmen on the opposing side to give me experience. This girl had always been excellent at games. The power in her shoulders and arms outmatched us all, and her stocky build and huge calf muscles made her a formidable opponent. When the time came for her to bat I was very frightened. I have always hated risking myself and I knew that she was very angry with me because she felt, as did the rest of the team, that in gaining my place I had usurped the favour of the games mistress. She hunched her shoulders over the bat and glowered at me. The afternoon sun shone and her shadow stretched towards me, and then the ball came flying down the pitch, and she swung straight at me. I instinctively raised my hands and caught the ball, swinging with it to lessen the pain. The crowds of girls and staff who were watching clapped and cheered, and I stood there foolishly grinning. They liked me. They were cheering for me because they cared for me, and I knew that I must not let 'them' down.

'She' was replaced by another 'bat', and the same thing happened again. They were determined to teach me a lesson. I knew that I had either to duck and risk losing the warm admiration of the school or catch the ball. If I missed, I risked having my nose smashed, or even my jaw shattered, for by now it had become a battle between the batsmen and myself. After the first over, I realized the spectators fully appreciated the pain and danger I was in; they had that familiar hot, glazed look in their eyes that I had seen all over the world—when the human turns into the animal and lusts for the kill. It was always hard to bowl Joan out, the opponent now batting, and my hands had become lumps of raw meat, swollen from the catches and split and bleeding.

I held on until the light failed and the match ended. I was a heroine. The crowds surged round me, hands patted me, and everyone said 'Well done'. Like an echo those words followed me back into the school, and then into the nearest bathroom, where I locked the door with great difficulty, because my hands were so swollen. I turned on the bath tap and let the cold water run over my hands, and then I was able to cry loudly, the noise masked by the rush of the water. I cried for a long time, because I needed to be loved by the people I lived with, but I knew that I was not like them. I was ashamed of myself for allowing my need for their approval to put me in a position where I needlessly damaged my hands, and risked a shattered face. I decided that I would not play cricket any more, or even compete against other people, because in all competition between human beings someone had to play the role of victor and someone else the role of vanquished, and both were ultimately damaged.

I said nothing to anyone, and on the day of the match I went missing. I sat all afternoon in the woods, imagining the crack of the ball on the wood. I could see myself gracefully diving for the ball in a perfectly held catch, and hear the warm loving roar of applause. I knew that if I had played cricket that day, I would have played for the crowd, and risked pain and bruises, when in my inner self I believed it was quite wrong. Going back to school after the match was very hard. It was assumed that I had chickened out. The faces were set, hard and cold, but I did not bother to explain. From then on, I reverted to being totally hostile and badly behaved.

We had heard that my mother was coming back to England for the summer holidays, and by the time she arrived, I had spent several weeks in 'Coventry'. No one was allowed to speak to me, and I spent my time either sitting in the library, eating my meals outside the dining room, or in bed. Thus, it was felt, I would be unable to corrupt any of the other girls. It was probably an effective way of controlling me. However, I lived my own interior life, and the days passed like a film before my eyes. The eyes behind my eyes filled with tears, filled with pain, and I longed for real human contact, but my public eyes were hard and clear like blue marbles.

My sister was ill most of the time at school, but now she had started suddenly to get thinner and thinner, and would sleep for hours. The nuns called in a doctor for her, but he could find nothing wrong. She seemed to be dying rapidly without giving any signals. My mother must have been a little shocked when she saw her, and learned at the same time, because I told her, that no one at school was allowed to speak to me. She tackled the nuns crossly on what had been happening to us while she was away. Questioned about me, in my presence, Mother Madeleine's thin lips disappeared altogether, and she began a litany of my faults. I watched fascinated as two bright red spots appeared on my mother's cheeks: it was a rare experience to see her anything but sunny and childlike. They argued for quite a while, and the upshot was that my mother said she was going to take my sister away since she was so far behind in her lessons, but that I had to remain until the end of term to take the G.C.E. exams; after that I would never darken their doors again.

The nuns agreed to let me stay because my mother had threatened to ask awkward questions about their educational standards, and I remained without my sister, after extracting a promise from my mother that I could leave on the day my final exam was over. On that day I was packed and ready to go when I saw Mother Madeleine gliding towards me. I knew she was going to go into the 'Well done' routine again. Despite all the pain and suffering she had caused me, we were supposed to shake hands and mutter 'No hard feelings'. She finally trapped me at the end of the corridor. In one hand she held a holy picture and a sacred medal. I dropped on to one knee and busied myself with my shoe laces. I would not look up or speak to her, and finally she felt foolish directing a stream of words at my bent head and glided away. I went home.

My mother told us that she had come home to have a small operation done in our local cottage hospital by our family doctor. We accepted that she was not very well, and she did look a little tired and preoccupied, but she soon settled into English life again, and my brother joined us for the summer holidays. My sister began to recover, and my mother decided that if she was tutored sufficiently, she should be able to pass her exams. So she was sent to a tutor in Lyme Regis, a very kindly man and an able teacher. But there was little he could do in the short time available: apart from all the basic ground rules of English and maths that my sister had blocked out, she was so crippled emotionally that she was unable to write anything down. Still she was pushed and prodded by my mother to repeated failure in exams she had no hope of passing. My brother was equally backward; he was virtually unable to read and his spelling was as bizarre as mine. It was my job to sit and teach him to read, which led to furious rows between us, and it was obvious that my mother was deeply disappointed in us.

I was forced to take violin lessons from a cantankerous old lady, who rapped my knuckles with her bow if I made a mistake. We were also required to join the local tennis club, where we were supposed to meet 'nice young people'. They probably were very nice, but they were nothing like us. We were lonely and isolated in our house, though it was probably the best time we were ever to have with our mother. Friends she had known abroad came to visit, and they spent a lot of time talking about the good old days. A lot of old China hands seemed to have settled in that area. Their homes were always crammed with ivory figurines and blue-and-white bowls, the floors covered with Chinese carpets. The rooms smelt of rosewood, and the fat buddhas grinned from the corners.

I was watching my mother's face when the telegram arrived from my father saying he was coming home. Suddenly she lost her bubbling exuberance. She looked preoccupied once more and strained. I sensed that she did not want him to come. We certainly did not. Though we had not lived with him for long, we still remembered the rows and the fear of him in the house. The afternoon he was to arrive, my mother was cooking on the Aga in the kitchen. I could feel how tense she was. I said, 'You don't want him to come home, do you?' 'No,' she said. That was the only admission she ever made, until she was dying.

I went into the garden, with rage welling up inside me that he should threaten the little happiness we had had, and was the first to see the taxi coming up the road. We stood in the hall, and Father came through the front door with a big happy smile on his face. His huge frame filled the doorway, blotting out the sunlight that was streaming in. We all smiled at him and he bent down and put his arms round my mother, and sucked her lips with pleasure at being with her. I watched her respond, knowing that it disgusted her. He had brought presents for us all and was like a small boy, telling us jokes and trying to communicate with us. Every time he put his arms around my mother, she flinched and moved away. I noticed and I followed them about, worried for her safety.

Finally, we were sent to bed. I sat at the top of the stairs, listening. I had taken the kitchen knife to bed with me. As my parents came up to bed, I moved back into my room, which was next door to their large room, where they each had a bed. I waited until they had stopped moving about and then I crept quietly into the hall, and watched them through the large gap in the hinged side of the half-open door. I had the knife in my hand, and I knew that if my father tried to cross over to my mother's bed, I was going to rush in and stab him to death.

She was lying against her pillows, reading her book, the bedside light shining on her long auburn hair. He was lying flat on his back, staring up at the ceiling. He was wearing his striped flannel pyjamas, and he had taken out his false teeth. She was not really reading. The silence went on for a long time, and then he said, 'Can I come over and give you a cuddle?' My muscles ached with the tension of waiting to spring. Then she said, 'No, not tonight, I'm tired.' She put out her light, and turned her back to him. He still lay staring at the ceiling, as though the words had never been said.

I crept quietly back into my room, and put the knife away in a drawer. I felt hugely elated, and heat raced from my body. I looked into the mirror and my eyes were blazing, and then I lay down and waited for my heart to stop pounding. Gusts of hatred swept over me. I heard my father begin to snore. Huge crescendos rolled round the house from the top floor. Great snorting silences, followed by long-range thunder, volleyed round my head. It was such a familiar noise, and now I resented it. It spoke of his absolute dominance. Even in sleep he was the invader. It was hours before I slept, but when I woke up I heard him shuffling about next door. He was truly home.

My mother went into hospital for her 'little' operation. We did not see her until the day after it was done. When I went into the little private room, I was shocked to see her lying so still, and with a white gauze pad where her breast had been. It had been necessary to remove her whole breast and the glands under her arm. For many weeks she attended another hospital for radium treatment, which burned her skin and made her exhausted and miserable. During all this time she said very little to us about her illness.

While she was in hospital, we had to look after our father, who dominated the house entirely. His every wish was our command. If he ordered a cup of tea, it had to be carried to him, and put down beside him, and then stirred for him. If I forgot to stir the tea, a long lecture would begin to the effect that our role in life was to care for him. At mealtimes he would carry on an endless monologue, telling the same stories time and time again, but no one was allowed to interrupt. His table manners were appalling. He stuffed his mouth full and chewed noisily, particles of food escaping from his lips as he talked. He was always served first, and always given the best food. He was cruel at times, and would insist that we ate everything we were served. The three of us hated the fat on ham or chops, but even if we gagged, we had to eat it because once he had been short of food as a child. We were much too frightened to argue with him. His only way of talking to us was in a bullying manner. Often he would give us lists of words, or poems, or dates in history which he felt we should know, thanks to our expensive education, and when we did not, the joking manner suddenly became menacing, as he worked himself up into a frenzy of recrimination. And then he would begin his litany of boyhood deprivation: the holes in his trousers, the bare feet . . . and the spittle would gather at the corners of his mouth, and we would stand silently waiting for something to distract him.

He began to insist that he should be allowed into the bathroom while we were having a bath, because it was 'his' house. If one of us forgot to replace the lavatory roll, he would line the three of us up and grill us. He was so unpredictable that we never knew quite what would set him off. He had no friends and no hobbies. He would read, but this meant skimming through a book with no concentration. The only time he was occupied was when he sat at his desk, doing endless sums and computations. My mother had money in Canada which brought in extra income, and, combined with his salary, they were really quite comfortably off; but his childhood had left him with a permanent fear of bankruptcy, and any bill would send him into a frenzy. His voice would rise to a high nagging pitch as he ranted on about the cost of living, or rushed to his desk to write out long columns of figures to prove doom and disaster were about to close in on us.

The hundred cigarettes he smoked a day gave him a dreadful cough and sinus trouble. My sister and I had to boil his disgusting handkerchiefs in salt water, and, as he still kept to the belief that baths were weakening, we had to deal with his very soiled underclothes. One day, when I was trying to wash a particularly revolting pair of socks for him, my sister broke down in the kitchen and said that she could not stand living with him any longer. Through all these awful times, there was a curious conspiracy of silence about what was really happening to us. On the surface, we moved about the house quite normally. When my mother was at home, she took the brunt of his bad moods, and we stayed out of the way. She never talked to us about his behaviour, or tried to explain why he behaved as he did—he was our father and he was omnipotent. Now, when I saw my sister crying, I suggested to her that we should just get rid of him.

The only methods I knew seemed fairly simple. The first we tried was ground glass. I ground it down very finely with a mortar and pestle and sprinkled it on an individual steak-and-kidney pie that he was having for supper. The meal was a nightmare, for we did not know what ground glass did to the human body. Would he fall to the ground and lie twitching, with blood pouring from every orifice, or would he die during the night? Nothing at all happened. We decided a week later that he was impervious to ground glass and another method must be found.

Next, we put shreds of tobacco into his tea, because my sister had a vague memory that it was deadly poison if taken with any liquid. She carried the tea to his side, the cup rattling so hard in her hand that she thought she would never get it there. He was sitting as usual in the big armchair, scratching the top of his head with his fingers and whistling through his teeth, gazing into space. He took a mouthful of the tea and spat it out. He said it tasted dreadful, and sent her into the kitchen to get some more. We had failed again.

By this time we were getting desperate, so we decided to tie a dressing-gown cord across the stairs late one night after he had gone to bed, and when the stairwell was in the shadows. My sister was to stand in the kitchen and scream loudly. He would, we hoped, race down the stairs, trip over the cord, and break his neck. This seemed very likely to work. When the night came, I saw him come up to bed, and we crept downstairs. I tied the cord. My sister screamed. He charged straight through the cord, which snapped without his even noticing it, and my sister was left trying to explain why she was screaming. We gave up after that, reluctantly deciding that he was indestructible.

Although the methods we used were childlike, our intent was deadly serious. To set about deliberately to kill requires such determination, and the arousing of such rage, that it scars you for life. You are like a piece of elastic that has been stretched too far, and will never regain its shape. From then on, I knew that I was capable of murder. Most human beings never reach that pitch, but I have talked to many mothers who, with their children, have tried to kill their partners. At the refuge we know what they have had to tolerate, and are not shocked—or are shocked only that an indifferent and uncaring society allow this sort of human drama to take place.

SIX

Dakar

I ALWAYS LOVED the cargo ships that took us back and forth across the world, discharging freight at exotic ports, carrying a completely safe, reliable world within their steel hulls. The ship's doctors were always alcoholic. The captain was always choleric, and the first mate always seduced as many of the wives who were on their own as he could, in the fastest way possible. My mother's main preoccupation, on first arriving on a ship, was to check the passenger list for suitable friends, and then to see if we were at the captain's table, and if not, why not. Once having sorted this little matter out with the purser in a way that left him bemused by her charm, she installed herself in her cabin—first class, of course.

We were on our way to Dakar, my sister and I on a ship with my mother; my brother had stayed behind at school in England, and my father had flown on ahead. There is a marvellous moment at sea when the water changes from a dull grey to a bottomless blue, when the sun starts to beat down on the deck and pale faces begin to grow pink, and everyone on the ship starts to relax and expand. The only passengers on our ship were women going out to their husbands. Many were leaving England for the first time, going to distant postings, leaving their children and all their roots behind. My mother was a mine of information on the life they would be leading, and spent hours counselling them. The voyage ended all too quickly, and we arrived in Dakar on a bright, hot day to see my father waiting on the quay.

The British Consulate in Dakar stood in a large garden surrounded by mango trees. The fruit, when it became ripe, sploshed on to the ground, and I spent the first few weeks sticky with juice and happiness to be away from England and school. The building was foursquare, big and rambling, the rooms full of heavy Victorian furniture. It was a monument to a forgotten age, and contrasted sharply with the gleaming white, modern city built by the French. Though my father was acting Consul General, we did not move into the huge old house; he preferred to live in a flat nearby, in order to save money. The flat, on the fourth floor, was very small, with only two bedrooms, a sitting room, kitchen and bathroom. So we were in his company far too much, and, while we were getting old enough to hate him a little less, the constant bickering and my mother's tears made it all hard to bear. It would have been much better if we had lived in the consulate, for then there would have been more space to keep away from him.

Because of my father's position, my mother had a lot of entertaining to do in Dakar. She was a very good hostess and much liked by all the staff and the foreign community. The same was not true of my father, who managed to antagonize everyone he came across, but because they were fond of her, they tolerated him—except for the Swiss Consul, who was as awkward and temperamental as he was. On Sundays, when the foreign community came to play tennis on our court, we would watch the unedifying spectacle of the two men accusing each other of cheating, throwing their tennis racquets to the ground and stalking off the court. In fact they both cheated, and were forced to play together so that they could bore each other with their monologues without ruining the party.

My father was incapable of holding a rational discussion in a group of people. If anyone contradicted him he took it as a personal insult, and would usually launch into an embarrassing attack on the offender. If this happened at a dinner party, the room would fall silent. People would stop eating and stare at him, but once he had had his say he would blithely continue to shove food into his mouth and then, looking up, he would ask why everyone was so quiet. We were not asked out socially very often because of his behaviour, though because we both felt an instinctive urge to protect or defend him, however badly he behaved, my sister and I never indicated that we thought he was anything other than perfect. People had to ask us on formal occasions, of course, and then my mother would be very careful not to upset him just before we went, because he would take malicious pleasure in embarrassing her in front of her friends.

I think my father felt very insecure in the company of middle-class English people, whose easy, outgoing charm he bitterly resented. He had seen many of his contemporaries in the Foreign Office promoted over his head because, or so he believed, they had been to University and had the background he lacked. He was in certain ways more gifted than many of them; his ability to record and collate information, his grasp of the political and economical situation in his area was first-class. But he was unable to see that his anti-social behaviour held him back, for he had very little insight into his own character. In Dakar, for the first time, I began to feel very sorry for him and to realize that, while my mother was charming and lovable, she did nothing to reassure him when he was insecure.

I must have been about fifteen when I first began to feel compassion for my father. In the subsequent events of my life, I lost any feeling I had for him; but one night, when one of the first little boys who came to the refuge had gone up to bed in tears, I followed the boy and asked him what was the matter. He looked at me and then, dropping his head, as if admitting a shameful act, he whispered, 'I miss my dad'. For a moment I could not think of anything to say. That child had been far worse treated than I. He had been beaten most cruelly, and his mother had nearly died from his father's beatings on several occasions; his handicapped brother had been kicked all around the sitting room, and yet this little boy cried for his dad. I hugged him and said, 'Of course you miss him—it's only right for you to miss your dad. Tell me about the nice things you used to do together.' His face lit up and he managed to remember a few good times. Ever after that I have made a point of letting children tell me about their fathers' good points.

Quite soon, in Dakar, my mother decided that we must continue our education. With her usual lack of understanding, she decided that we were going to attend the University of Dakar, largely because it sounded socially acceptable. 'My daughters are both at University' came easily to her lips. She contacted a friend of hers who was in a position to arrange a place for us at the University in return for a few social invitations. We were bundled into the car and our driver instructed to take us there. We stood in the hallway, holding hands, as the students milled around us. Most of them were African; there were perhaps fifty French students in the whole complex. All sessions were in French, a language neither of us could speak.

The segregation was rigid, which surprised me. At St Mary's, and at our school, there had been many students from abroad, but as most of them came from ruling families and were usually the richest children in the place, they were rarely discriminated against. So it was not until I went to Africa that I discovered racial prejudice in its full reality. There were no black women at all at the University, and those I was to see around the campus were the local prostitutes. I liked all the students, but the black students in our class were particularly kind to me. I soon learnt to speak French fluently, but they were forced to struggle through Keats's 'Ode on a Grecian Urn', which seemed particularly inappropriate in the middle of Africa, where Grecian urns are rather hard to come by. I began to give informal English lessons and to get to know many of the students. It was only one day when I walked into the huge dining room, with its separate tables for blacks and whites, and sat down next to a black friend of mine instead of joining my French friends, that I understood the potential explosiveness of the situation. The whole room became silent, and my friend said quietly, 'You had better go back to your own table.' 'But why?' I asked. 'Because,' he said. Shamefaced, I got up and walked back to the white table. The room immediately resumed its chatter. The French students did not explain. But I had been warned that it would be dangerous for me to try to integrate. I accepted it.

My mother, meanwhile, was very busy with her bridge parties, which were held in rotation in certain selected houses. The parties at our flat were not very successful, largely thanks to my marmoset. He was the joy of my life; I loved his wizened little face and soft grey fur, and was astonished at the enormity of his genitals. Unfortunately, he vented his lust upon any woman who came into the flat. As soon as the good ladies sat down, he would perch on top of the curtain rail, calling loudly for attention, and sit bolt upright to expose to best advantage his prize possession. Once acknowledged, he would proceed to masturbate furiously. If they ignored him, in the best English fashion, he would quietly get under the table and choose an inviting leg to stroke. I always enjoyed the expression of horror on a matronly face when she felt five minute fingers clasping her ankle, and on bending down, gazed into Ti-Ti's lascivious brown eyes. The ladies soon agreed to play bridge elsewhere, which suited me. It meant an end to the non-stop gossip and the chore of handing out tea and sweetmeats.

Ti-Ti soon took possession of the whole flat. He would only go to bed at night, when I produced his rolled-up blanket in his box. The rest of the time he plagued my family and the servants. My father hated him, and the feeling was reciprocated; the two of them kept up a running battle. As soon as my father returned from the office, the servant brought him a tray of tea. If, by any chance, the 'boy' forgot to put out a dish of milk for the monkey beside the tea tray, Ti-Ti would dash down from the curtain rail and bite my father. My father would leap to his feet with a roar of rage, roll up his airmail copy of *The Times* and proceed to chase the monkey around the flat. The monkey made it his business to take refuge under sofas or behind projecting ledges so that my father, trying to swipe at him, would sustain severe head injuries. The servants and the family would look on helplessly until, worn out, my father would sink into his chair and there would be peace for a short while. It would only last until dinner, when Ti-Ti, sitting on the curtain rail nearest to the table, would decide that he particularly liked the meat being served. He would wait until my father had lovingly loaded his fork and was about to put it into his mouth; then, like a flash, he would land on the table, grab the fork in his paw, and jump back on to the curtain rail, chewing triumphantly, before my father registered what had happened.

Very soon, I was told to find another home for Ti-Ti. He was such an outrageous little creature that we pleaded to be allowed to keep him, but even my mother, who was usually very lenient about animals, was adamant. It was true that he smelt awful, and when she had her afternoon rest, he would creep into her room, and lie in her long tresses of hair, rubbing them carefully all over his body and under his little arms. She slept deeply and it would take quite a time before his familiar and awful smell permeated her dreams, and she would rouse and chase him from the room.

The marmoset's great enemies were the vultures, who circled the block of flats, clacking down from the sky to sit on the dustbins and peck at the refuse. They massed in groups, wagging their long fleshy pink necks, plotting to capture him. He would lie on the balcony railings, quite confident that the overhang from the flat above would protect him from their swooping attacks. All day, he would hurl abuse at them, and they would circle and swoop at him, until, one day, he got so overconfident and excited that he fell off. I watched him fall and as he fell, he stretched out his arms and legs and almost floated to the ground. I raced downstairs and found him breathless but unhurt, but he was so put out by the loss of face that he bit me fiercely as I carried him upstairs. The bite was deep into my finger, and it soon became very red and swollen and streaks appeared up my arm. My mother ignored my tears and said it would heal on its own. When it did not, she put my hand under the cold tap, and pierced the swollen hand with a needle. The relief was enormous, but the hurt at her callousness remained.

Part of my mother's day was spent at the local hospital, rolling bandages with other women from the various consulates. It was a social occasion and I preferred not to have to sit there making dressings for the patients. Another equally unexciting job was visiting any sick English people in the French hospital. These patients were usually young boys who had run away from home in England, in an attempt to join the Foreign Legion; they had probably stowed away on a ship and been put off at Dakar, exhausted and starving, for the British Consulate to return home. Or they were Englishmen who had run away from the Foreign Legion, once they had discovered that it was a living hell, and ended up in hospital with sunstroke after their journey across the desert. It never entered my mother's mind that two fifteen-year-old girls could not easily play social worker to these very distressed men, so we would sit mutely by their beds, while they sobbed and talked of home.

Finally, we were so rude about Mother's good works that she sent us to help out at a clinic for mothers and children, run by a missionary doctor outside Dakar. We arrived to see two wooden huts on the edge of a village surrounded by a sixteen-foot wire fence. We walked through the gates into the first hut where we met Miss Werter. She was about thirty years old, wore modern clothes, and seemed to have a marvellous sense of humour. The mothers and children came to her from the village with their illnesses or problems, and she did her best to help them. This did not please the local village medicine man, who promptly put a curse upon her. Just as we arrived the atmosphere had become very tense. Miss Werter had been away for two weeks in the city, and her replacement had decided to have a 'Bonny Baby' competition. One of the prizes had been a bar of soap, which the grateful mother had fed to her baby, who died of convulsions. This had pleased the witch doctor no end. Miss Werter had a great faith in God, and despite such setbacks, she and another woman missionary continued to work with the villagers. They did not ram religion down the mothers' throats, and they were regarded by the mothers with amused tolerance because they had never had a man. The village women's comments about us were ribald in the extreme.

My sister enjoyed going to help at the clinic, but I found the sewing and knitting classes too reminiscent of school, so I stuck to attending University, when I felt like it. Gradually, I made some French friends who invited us to parties. By now, going on sixteen, I considered myself very sophisticated. I taught myself to smoke by taking one of my father's large tins of Players and smoking solidly through the lot, until I could inhale without coughing and spluttering. And I was getting quite good at chatting about nothing at the many official parties.

When the biggest official event of the year—the Queen's Birthday Party, to which all the British subjects were invited—came round, my mother was ill, too ill even to dictate orders from her sickbed, and I was instructed to see to the arrangements. The servants had done it all before, so I assumed they would know what to do. Invitations were sent out to all the local dignitaries. On the day, the men arrived elegantly besuited, and the women in beautiful cocktail dresses. Unfortunately, however, I had forgotten to restrict the Muslim guests to one wife each. Very soon the huge reception room began to fill with African women dressed in layers of multi-coloured cloth, wearing turbans, and carrying their babies. Most of the Africans who had received my invitation would ordinarily have appeared with only their 'town' wives, who were city girls, probably more sophisticated than I was. However, on this occasion the village wives obviously did not want to miss the chance of a good party, so they came as well. The servants carried round great platters of 'small eats'. Most of the wives had arranged themselves on the little spindly gold chairs lining the walls and they were busy sticking their huge brown nipples into the mouths of babies who were, by now, crying loudly to be fed. When the food arrived the wives took huge handfuls of sandwiches and chatted and laughed raucously with their friends. The drink began to circulate, and I, of course, had not realized that Muslims are not permitted to drink. I had to send out for more orange squash, because everyone wanted it neat. Looking across the long room, I thought it looked more like a marketplace than the British Consulate. The offended white guests were clustered together, trying to make themselves heard over the hubbub of the women. My father never noticed the confusion at all. He continued to move amiably round the room, much more at home than I had ever seen him before. He did not tell my mother, but I knew, after this, that I would never be a good hostess.

We were beginning to receive invitations to tea at select French homes. Young girls of good family in Dakar would invite each other to formal tea parties, and as we were part of the diplomatic corps, we were included. Our first invitation came from the daughter of the High Commissioner, and it was to lunch at the magnificent palace in which they lived. My mother was ecstatic. My sister and I were washed and combed and delivered to the door, after passing fierce-looking Senegalese guards who stamped their feet and saluted us. We went up in the lift to the top floor, where we stepped into a perfectly empty room with a table laid for three. The view over Dakar and the sea was panoramic. At length, a girl came through a door at the far end of the room and across the floor towards us. She was nearly as shy as we were. She must have had polio, because her legs were in calipers. We stood and looked mutely at each other.

She beckoned to us to sit down, and a servant glided in and served the first course. It was a plate of unpeeled prawns, with a wedge of lemon on the side. I looked desperately at my sister. We had never encountered prawns before. The three of us sat in silence. I bowed my head and began to crunch my way through the pile on my plate. My sister, in a strangled voice, said that she was allergic to shellfish, and left them on her plate. I shot a few secret glances at our hostess to see how she was handling her prawns. She seemed to be swallowing them whole, as if by magic, without leaving a trace. I got through as many of the things as I could and then I heard a crunching sound from beneath the table. I lifted the cloth to see a large cat at our hostess's feet, working its way through a pile of shells. 'I don't like them,' she said, by way of explanation. 'Neither do I,' I said, pushing the plate away. 'Do you always eat them whole?' she asked. 'Always,' I said, firmly. We were never invited again, and it did not take long for the rest of the social set to decide that we were not *'comme il faut'*—much to our relief, and much to our mother's disappointment.

My father's eighteen months' posting in Dakar was coming to an end—too soon for me. I loved Africa and the people who lived there. I still found it difficult to accept the poverty, though food was plentiful because there were so many mango trees, and paw-paws, lemons, breadfruit, bananas and pineapples were to be had for the picking. Dakar was a joyful city. Everywhere you walked you would see cheerful women gossiping and selling food. Their children would suddenly start to clap their hands and break into complicated dances on the street corners. The vitality of the city rose to greet you as you wandered round the busy markets, with great slabs of meat piled high on the counters, crawling with flies, and fruit arranged in glowing pyramids around the women squatting on their haunches. The flower stalls exploded with colour, and the women flower-sellers would shake with laughter as they enquired into your private life.

There were lovely beaches round the city, and we would spend hours lolling by the warm sea, listening to 'The Desert Song', as I imagined the handsome sheik who would sweep me off my feet and take me with him into his tent. I was still a little vague about what might happen there, but an elderly guest at the Consulate must have felt my yearnings, because when I went swimming with him, he spent the afternoon making grabs at me in the water. He was definitely not my idea of the ultimate experience, and I fended him off as best I could.

A few weeks later we were swimming on a fairly isolated beach, when a group of French soldiers, about fifteen of them, got into the water behind us. They swam towards us, and the look of naked lust in their eyes really terrified us and we began to swim out to sea.

French servicemen had a dreadful reputation for rape and violence, and we swam as fast as we could. My sister, who was never a strong swimmer, gave up and started sinking, but I, electrified by fear, must have beaten the world record. As soon as the soldiers caught up with my sister they must have realized that she was English, and that they would be in dire trouble if they touched her. Then they were faced with the awful possibility that I might have drowned, and they would somehow be blamed. They began to shout reassuringly to me that they would not hurt me, and finally I stopped. They swam out and helped me ashore, assuring me that they had not intended to hurt us. Once ashore, they became ordinary, kindly men, but I knew that if we had been French girls, or black girls, we would not have stood a chance. Again I had seen faces transformed by violence. It took me a long time to recover from the fear of that day.

SEVEN

England Again: Streatham and Bridport

THE TAXI DROVE through the rain-soaked streets past long rows of squat suburban houses. 'It can't be one of these,' I said nervously to my mother. 'Of course not, he was a professor,' she said, sounding less than confident. She was wrong. The taxi drew up in front of the fifty-sixth private hedge, and we got out and stood on the pavement, gazing bleakly at the house we had rented in England. It was the usual little suburban semi-detached house with a small garden. To my mother, it was a dreadful shock, but she had only herself to blame, as she had never bothered to enquire into the details when an English professor in Dakar had offered to let his house to us while we were in England. She had assumed that all professors live in elegant houses, and imagined Streatham to be a middle-class neighbourhood within ten minutes of Harrods. Now she felt bitterly betrayed.

We were all back in England for a short stay before my father took up his new posting in China. I felt very psychic about that, because we had been all packed and ready to leave Dakar for what we had been told would be our next post, Recife, in Brazil, when I had had a dream. In it I saw a letter saying that we were not going to Brazil, but back to China. 'Impossible,' said my mother when I told her about it. 'There is nowhere in China left to go.' But the day before we sailed for Brazil a telex arrived telling my parents to return to England and then to Macao in China—the last outpost.

So now, in Streatham, my mother stomped about the professor's house, removing the flying ducks from the walls and ripping off the net curtains so that our private lives lay exposed to the curious eyes of the neighbours. She engaged a charlady who stayed only three hours when she found that on top of all the cleaning, she was expected to bring my mother tea on a properly laid tray. She told my mother that she was not a servant, and slammed the door behind her so hard that the plates in the kitchen rattled. 'Definitely a communist,' said my mother firmly. It sounded an awful thing to be, because it was well known that communists cut off babies' heads, did not believe in God, and 'were everywhere'.

I was very happy in this little house. It felt safe and secure, and above all, it had a television set. This was the first time I had ever seen one, and I lay on the sofa in front of it in a blissful drugged stupor. I particularly loved the musicals. I can remember longing to join on the end of one of the chorus lines, smiling widely and swinging my legs. But one look at myself in the mirror was enough to bring me swiftly down to earth. I was a large spotty teenager, and, as my mother insisted on choosing our clothes, I was still dressed as a twelve-year-old, although I was now all of sixteen. In my mother's fantasy, we were still 'little girls'. Never mind the protruding breasts and massive calf muscles. She dressed my sister in blue and me in pink, in dresses with Peter Pan collars, tight little bodices and gathered skirts. We were both aware that we looked awful. We were not allowed to wear our hair in a fringe, because it was 'common', and there was no question of lipstick or nylons.

It never crossed my mother's mind that we might be interested in boys. Her only serious comment on the facts of life was a clipped conversation in which she informed me that girls who played with themselves found that their vaginas grew into massive cabbages. My sister and I both looked startled and she nodded wisely. Obviously pleased by the effect this piece of information had had upon us, she said that sex was all very well for the first three months of marriage, but thereafter it was a burden to be borne bravely by all wives. This fitted in rather neatly with what we had been told by the nuns at our school, and life began to look very bleak indeed. Fortunately, my mother made the mistake of allowing our cousin Michael to take us to the theatre in London, a revue whose contents she had not bothered to vet. There I saw women who sang freely of unlicensed sexual adventure. I checked carefully, and could see no evidence of cabbages marring the tight fit of their leotards, nor did the men look like emaciated skeletons, riddled with disease. Maybe, I thought, my mother was not the expert she claimed to be. Years later a little boy of ten came up to me at the refuge, saying

'People say that if I touch my eyeball . . . I will go blind.' I stopped what I was doing and looked at him. I knew this must have come from his mother, a very repressed woman. 'James,' said, 'you can touch any part of your body with your hands, and nothing will happen to you. Your body is designed to give you pleasure.' James looked visibly more relaxed. 'If I touch my eyeball, do you promise I won't go blind?' he asked. 'Go on, try it,' I said. Very gingerly, he did. He blinked a couple of times, then a huge grin came over his face, and he rushed off, delighted. I do not think his mother will have the same power over him again.

While we were in Streatham my father was away most of the day working at the Foreign Office. But the nights were hideous with quarrels over money. My mother had decided that as there was little provision for education in Macao, I should stay in England to do a secretarial course; my sister was to go with them to China and my brother would stay at school in England. As soon as she had chosen the secretarial college, at Bridport in Dorset, my mother took me to Harrods to buy 'suitable' clothes. The ones she chose were mostly highly unsuitable for the provincial town of Bridport, and my father exploded at the size of the bill. Between her extravagance and his meanness, there raged a never-ending battle. He would shout at her, becoming hysterical as he ranted on about the financial ruin that stared us in the face. She would sob uncontrollably, and we would sit silently in our rooms, hating him for making her cry. I hated myself as well, for being too frightened to defend her, but the rage that welled up inside me never showed on my face. My father's moods changed so quickly that I learned to anticipate, from the movements of his body and the look in his eyes as he came through the door, when he was about to explode. If he saw any hint of sympathy in our faces, he would turn on us and begin his childhood reminiscences once again. Tears would pour down his cheeks as we watched disgusted.

My father hired a car to drive me down to the college in Bridport, and we set off with the whole family in tow. We broke down about six times on the way. This was not unusual, as my father tortured any car he drove. He drove as though his was the only car on the road, very slowly down the middle on the white line, and felt personally insulted if anyone dared to overtake him. The cars behind him crunched steadily into each other, as signalling was beyond him, but he had a clean driving licence, so he believed that he was an excellent driver. We had to grit our teeth and shut our ears to the offended hooting that followed our progress wherever we went.

On the way to Bridport we shuddered to a halt halfway down a steep hill, of course in the middle of the road. My father got out and lifted the bonnet and gazed thoughtfully at the engine. 'It must be the sparking-plugs,' he said knowledgeably. (It was always the fault of the sparking-plugs, because that was the limit of his knowledge of the engine's anatomy.) He began to busy himself with the leads. I noticed that he had a large hole in the seat of his trousers. Cars piled up behind us. When one driver got out and suggested he push the car to the side of the road, he glared at the man, who drew back. My father was a big man. He returned to inspecting the engine. 'The man's a fool,' said the driver standing beside me. 'He's not a fool,' I said furiously. 'He's my father.' Even I was surprised at the the ferocity of my response.

At last we arrived at the college and I said goodbye to my family. It was back to dormitory life, and the grind of shorthand and typing. The first night, unpacking in the dormitory, I hung up the unsuitable clothes. 'You won't want that sort of thing here,' one of the girls said. 'I know,' I said, looking at the jeans and jerseys the other girls wore. My mother did not believe any nice girls wore trousers. She was so far out of touch with reality that she had made no financial provision for me while I was alone in England, beyond £12 a month for 'extra expenses', which was to be paid into my account in a local bank. I had never handled money before—my only experience had been the 2s 6d I had received as pocket money at school and at St Mary's—and almost immediately I overdrew at the bank in order to buy some decent clothes. I then opened accounts at all the shops in the area and the debts mounted up, while the fear of what would happen when my father found out haunted me all the time I was at college.

The secretarial course was fairly easy, but with my dreadful spelling difficulties I soon found myself spending many hours in detention, trying to memorize long lists of words. It was useless. I could learn them one day and they would be gone the next. We had to do double-entry bookkeeping, and again, I found I was unable to do the simple arithmetic necessary to make books balance. I had never managed to get past adding and subtracting and even then I had to use my fingers to do the simplest sum. Because I was so articulate, my bad spelling and arithmetic were seen as acute laziness on my part, and I was punished accordingly. And so, yet again, I was bottom of the class, and a failure.

The first term ended, and two of the senior girls who had graduated and were going to London to get jobs invited me to spend a fortnight there with them. I was delighted. I spent the first part of the holiday at St Mary's and then took a train to London.

Joan and Rachel met me at the station and took me to their tiny bed-sitting rooms at the top of a bed-and-breakfast hotel in Bayswater. To me these were two of the most beautiful rooms in the world. The rest of the hotel was used by American Air Force officers on leave in London. The two girls had already picked out their own boyfriends, and they had thoughtfully supplied one for me. Called Joe, he was balding and middle-aged but very kind. I did not want to hurt his feelings by refusing his company, and on my first evening we all went out to a jazz club. The club was in a basement and the man on the door tried to refuse to let me in, because I was underage. I was humiliated and resolved at once to learn how to use make-up.

In the end the doorkeeper relented, and I got drunk for the first time in my life. I woke up next morning to find myself in Joe's bed. After the initial panic, I realized that we were both fully dressed. I checked and discovered that I still had my knickers on, and Joe woke up and looked at me very strangely and said that I should go home immediately. I explained that I did not actually have a home, that you had to book a place at St Mary's and that the college was closed. He heaved a great sigh. 'That's the first time I've slept with a man,' I said, feeling very worldly. 'I believe you,' he said with great feeling.

It was now obvious that the two girls intended to use their bed-sitting rooms for their boyfriends, so I was expected to share Joe's bed, which I did quite happily. He had two weeks' leave, and he took me all around London. At night we returned to the hotel and I would snuggle up to his big warm frame, feeling safe and secure. He never took his trousers off, but they were often suspiciously moist in the morning, and occasionally he would moan and thrash about. I was very curious, but once I discovered that he was married, I decided that he was keeping himself for his wife, which seemed a noble thing to do.

I had a marvellous time, and when it came to an end, we said goodbye and he cried. He said he was crying for me, which seemed very odd, as I was having such a good time. I waved to him as the train pulled out of the station. I never saw him again.

Back at college, I began to go down with sore throats. The doctor said I should have my tonsils out, and I was put into the local cottage hospital. The matron at the college took me over to the hospital the night before the operation, and I lay, terrified, in my bed. The only other occupant of the room was a very old lady who looked as if she was going to die, which did not help very much. I grew more and more frightened as the night went on and the nurse kept putting her head round the door to tell me to go to sleep, as I kicked and turned in the bed. Every time I got up to go to the lavatory, I disturbed her in a clinch with one of the male nurses, and they got very angry with me.

Finally it was time to put on the long hospital gown with the humiliating opening down the back, and then to have the pre-med injection. I lay behind my screen feeling my heart thumping, sure I would never come out of the operation alive. At lunchtime they came for me and put me on the trolley. I was wide awake and talking nineteen to the dozen. I was wheeled into the operating theatre, and they clamped a mask over my face and told me to count. One, two, three, and the room began to spin. Four, five, six, and all I could see were eyes, staring down through the kaleidoscope, and then nothing.

I woke up in my own bed. I was coughing. There was no one in the room except the old lady, who was asleep. Blood was trickling out of my mouth; then it came faster. I pressed the bell, but no one came. I tried to shout for help, but the great clots of blood in my throat choked my voice. The old lady opened her eyes and saw me covered in blood, and she stumbled from her bed, and began to scream on the landing: 'She's dying, she's dying!' A nurse came in and then my bed was surrounded by people injecting me, wrapping ice packs around my neck, trying to help me breathe. 'The surgeon's gone sailing,' I heard the sister say, in a desperate voice. Then someone was found, and I was wheeled back into surgery, fighting and struggling, to have the inside of my throat stitched up.

When I came to I was in a lot of pain. No one visited me and there was not a word from my parents, even though they knew I was in hospital. I refused to eat. I did not sleep. I was rude and hostile. When the surgeon did his rounds with the doctors and nurses, I turned my back on them, and would not speak to them. I wrote to my parents on the first day I came round, and told them that I had nearly died, and how frightened I had been, and how I loved and missed them. I waited and waited for a reply. At last one came from my father, a very long letter. He was very angry with me for upsetting my mother. He had had his tonsils taken out on a kitchen table, with an old pair of scissors and without anaesthetic. How dare I make a fuss? The rest of the letter was on the usual themes: my good fortune, thanks to his loving care, as compared with the misery and suffering of his own childhood.

I did not even cry. I was just ruder than ever, and when the matron of the college came to see me, because the hospital had complained to her about my bad behaviour, I told her to get lost. Finally, they let me go back to the college. After two days of staggering around I collapsed and the local doctor said that I must have iron injections, because I had lost so much blood. Every day I would catch the bus into town, because I was too weak to cycle, and the nurse would give me a massive injection into the vein in my arm, which would go blue and throb. Then I would catch the bus back.

I had two good friends at the college, both girls from Nairobi, and the three of us went everywhere together. The girls there who had grown up in England had a totally different attitude to life. Their horizons were limited strictly to having a job and then marrying. And although in a sense we were unsophisticated, so that boyfriends were of no interest to us, in another sense we had travelled so much and seen so many things that we made them feel provincial and they were hostile towards us. We three rode our bicycles all over the Dorset hills. We shared what we had and, because I had so little money and they had plenty, sent by their rich families in Africa, they often paid for me.

The summer term at Bridport was my last. Normally, one was

supposed to stay for a year, but my mother had decided that I would do the course in nine months. I was to fly out with my brother to join the family during the summer holidays. Of course, I was expected to pass my exams and get my diploma before I left. I had no hope of passing but it was possible that I could get a certificate for 120 words a minute in shorthand, and 45 words a minute typing. The typing was no problem, but the shorthand seemed doubtful, so I made a plan to pretend to take down the dictation during the final test, ask to go to the lavatory, where I would complete it, and then give it in. It worked. The teacher let me go, as I urgently whispered that I had a bad period, and needed to change, and I sauntered back, handed in my paper and passed. Many failed. I pitied them for not finding a way round the system. But 'Thou shalt not cheat' was engraved on their souls.

EIGHT

Macao and Hong Kong

THE DESCENT TO the airport at Hong Kong was almost vertical, and I passed out. The three-day flight which my brother and I had made from London, on a special plane carrying children to the Far East to join their parents, had been a nightmare. I had a bad cold, and was in agony with ear-ache; whenever we landed or took off, the stewardess crouching beside me holding a hot-water bottle to my ear would wince as I screamed with pain. How I longed for one of the safe, leisurely ships on which we had travelled in the past.

At Karachi the meal we were given had been contaminated, and all the passengers were ill, with vomiting and diarrhoea. But when we stumbled down the gangway at Hong Kong, exhausted and dishevelled, to find my mother and sister waiting to greet us, all my mother could talk about was a lunch party she had arranged to introduce us to the 'nice' girls in Hong Kong. Very important people were going to be there.

She whisked us away to the hotel to wash and change, chattering all the way across the city in the taxi. I looked at my sister, and was shocked to see how thin she was. She did not look at all happy. The lunch at a hotel was a nightmare. My mother grew very angry with me as I sat white-faced at the table, almost deaf and in pain. She leant over and hissed 'Noblesse oblige' at me. I had told her about the journey, but she dismissed it all with a wave of her hand. She had arranged to show us off to her friends and we were not to let her down. I did my best, and when the lunch was over we got into the ferry that would take us across to Macao, where my father was waiting for us.

As we sat on the stern deck, watching the island of Hong Kong disappear behind us, and the mainland of Communist China loom up ahead, huge junks creaked past the ferry and small squat gunboats hovered like gnats, patrolling the narrow straits. The crossing was always precarious, because the gunboats belonged to the Communists, who patrolled the waters, searching for Chinese who disliked life on the mainland and were trying to escape to Hong Kong. Sometimes refugees managed to bribe their way on to a junk, which would then be stopped and searched; or else the pirates who also lurked in the islands would decide to raid one of the junks, and the guards on the boats would take to their guns. It was all very exciting to a pasty-faced girl just out of England.

Slowly the outline of Macao harbour appeared. My sister pointed out our house which stood at the water's edge—a large white wedding-cake of a building, with a flagpole flying the Union Jack. The city of Macao squatted on mud flats which lay exposed most of the day except when the tide rose sufficiently to allow the boats in and out of the harbour. The smell of the mud in the estuary was dark and cloying for many months of the year, a smell which stuck to your body and lay in your hair. But the city was beautiful and I fell in love with it the moment I stepped on to the shore.

In such a small city our arrival was national news. We were bustled off the boat and into a waiting car and swept away down the long meandering road that ran alongside the sea to our house. The driver did a corkscrew turn that brought us to the front door. High wire fences surrounded the house. Everywhere lay the threat of death. Macao was the gold centre of the East, the gambling centre, the listening-post to China, and it was split up into warring factions of gangsters. The brooding silence contained an element of violence which prickled the skin and made one constantly alert. Next door to us lived a millionaire's daughter under heavy guard, in case of kidnapping, and always I was aware of the chunky figures of her guards who lolled around the gardens, occasionally relieving their boredom by taking pot shots at the geckos, or any other moving animal.

Our nice house, it seemed, was haunted. It had belonged to a rice merchant who had made a vast profit during the war by hoarding grain. Finally the people of Macao, who were starving, had come up to the house to kill him. While they were massing round the gates, he was seen pacing up and down the flat roof, and then he died of a heart attack before they got to him. He had cursed the

house before he died and no one would live there; but the Foreign
Office, with typical English phlegm and a nice sense of economy,
rented it cheaply for their consuls. Sometimes at night you could
hear quite clearly the footsteps on the roof, pacing up and down.
Our dogs would go rigid with fear, the hair on their spines stiffening,
and they would howl and snarl at the bottom of the stairs to the
roof; nothing would induce them to go up those stairs, and we would
lie uneasy in our beds waiting for the morning.

On my first morning in Macao, I awoke to the sound of creaking
and groaning outside my window. I walked out on to the veranda
and saw the huge junk fishing fleet sail by, magnificently painted
and looking like an armada of Spanish galleons setting out for war.
The wind caught them and they swept past me, their sails billow-
ing and swelling, into deeper water, leaving a calm sea with a view
of the island of Colowan across the straits.

Our life together as a family began again. After breakfast, served
by Ah Lei, the best cook in Macao, and beginning with large wedges
of glowing paw-paw, followed by toast and English marmalade, my
father would leave for the Consulate office near by, come back at
lunchtime, have a sleep, and then return to work for the remainder
of the afternoon. At 6 p.m. he would return, listen to the B.B.C.
overseas news, and then the whole family would be driven with the
two dogs to a small hill, where we would walk for half an hour.
We would return home, wait for dinner, and then go to bed. No
television, no books, no libraries, no English people. The colony was
Portuguese, with rigid rules of behaviour. All the young people lived
and worked in Hong Kong and the only social life was bridge, cocktail and dinner parties, made fluent by heavy and sweet Portuguese
wine. I did not like anyone at all.

No wonder my sister was wasting away. I dragged her off into the
city to explore. The rickshaws were attached to bicycles, and we
sat together, being pedalled about by old men with calf muscles
seamed with bursting blue veins, grunting and groaning as they
pulled us round the back streets which were teeming with people.
We spent hours in cramped joss-filled shops looking for smuggled
treasure from the mainland. We explored the ruined cathedral, whose
façade looked like the entrance to the theatre of life, so that when
you walked through the huge arch into the flattened waste land

beyond, you were on stage and no longer a dispossessed alien but a reincarnation of another age. We sat in the English churchyard reading the legends on gravestones of missionaries, seamen, babies and a few dignitaries who had come to Macao, only to die of some tropical disease. The white, bloated faces of the drowned sailors, pressed into the earth by heavy marble stones, haunted me.

Late at night, the gambling house would open. Fan-tan, poker and roulette were the main games. Every floor ran a different game, and on the eighth floor were the whores, who glided through the gambling house like painted cats, their cheongsams split up the side to their waist. Some nervous tourists would find themselves swept away, and were sometimes disgorged days later, having gambled all their money away, fornicated away all their inhibitions, to find themselves slightly shamefacedly making their way back on the ferry to Hong Kong, muttering promises not to go again—but they did. It was all marvellously exotic to a young girl. The city encapsulated all that was evil, yet displayed its seductive wares with such showmanship that they seemed acceptable.

A handful of famous Chinese ran the syndicates of Macao. Ho Yin owned the gold concession. He also owned six wives. Every year, he held a party for the Macao 'Grand Prix', when his gardens were opened and tables set out to feed the rich and famous. There were lobsters sitting on thrones made of ice, with wheels of prawns and hillocks of caviar flanking the thrones. Guests would wander among the trees, drinking champagne, and Ho Yin, who was also the Communist representative in Macao, would watch them with hooded eyes. He was a very gentle and kind man who loved his first wife very dearly. He took me to the vault in the city where the gold was stored. In the dingy room, I saw hundreds of bricks of gold, worth millions and millions of pounds, neatly stacked against the walls. Ho Yin said I could have a brick if I could carry it to the door. I could not begin to lift it, and he laughed and gave me a necklace instead.

Other Chinese ran the gambling syndicates. The most famous of them all had been kidnapped and held for a huge sum of money as ransom; when his relatives were slow in paying up, they were sent half his ear through the post. When I sat next to this man I would natter nervously, goggling at the mutilated ear. Before I arrived in

Macao he had been ambushed again. This time the British Consul (the one my father had succeeded) had been with him, and was forced to take refuge behind a hedge while a machine-gun raked the car, killing the driver. A bullet passed through the Consul's panama hat, so that he had had to send for a replacement from the Army & Navy Stores.

There was also the firecracker king, who came for drinks one day. A few days later, lying in bed, I heard gunshots, and learnt that he had died that night.

We entertained these Chinese gentlemen, but never their wives. The giving and receiving of hospitality was endlessly intricate. Our Chinese hosts would give huge banquets with countless courses, and we had to eat everything, at least a little of it, for fear of offending. Lumps of seaweed looming out of a brown sludge; sea slugs that blurted out inky salt into your throat; duck's feet chopped off at the ankles, lying limply on a plate—these were some of the 'delicacies' hardest to swallow. Some of the food was delicious, but I never enjoyed the meals because something exotically nasty was bound to turn up, and be offered by a proud and beaming host.

Present-giving at Christmas turned our house into Aladdin's cave. Chauffeurs would arrive at the front door and unload crates which we put under the tree. Silver tea sets, cigarette cases, tapestries, precious vases, jade, all this would be given. Our chance to reciprocate would be at the Chinese New Year, when we would send tea from Harrods, chocolates from Fortnums, biscuits from the Army & Navy Stores. Then good Anglo-Chinese relationships would reign for the rest of the year.

To while away the time between feasts and entertainments, we would take the boat to Colowan Island, to picnic and swim among the rich Portuguese, who had built holiday villas there. Next to Colowan lay a Communist island, and during our journey out, we would be followed by those sinister grey Communist gunboats. They made my flesh creep, remembering my mother's stories of children who reported their own parents, and were subsequently taken away and killed. Some yachts which had been blown off course in these waters were seized by the Communists, never to be seen again. On our way back, the shadows would grow long as the sun went down, and the crocodile shapes would glide behind us. The mainland ahead seemed to slumber, and behind it stretched a vast unknown territory in which lived millions of Chinese now destined to do the bidding of a tyrant called Mao, who did not believe in God. We had to be ever vigilant, we were told, because they were creeping closer and closer, and my father's job was to keep an eye on the situation for Whitehall.

In the event of a Communist invasion, which we were led to believe was always imminent, we had been allotted a small naval launch, which was to take us British subjects to Hong Kong at full speed. Orders were laid down that guns for our protection should remain in our house, but that the ammunition should be kept in the office a quarter of a mile away. The reason for the separation was bizarre: it was feared that in the event of a siege, the brain of the Consul would become addled by the extreme drama of the situation to such an extent that he might go berserk and shoot the servants, thereby causing a diplomatic embarrassment. We had to go through a practice evacuation, which was in itself deeply embarrassing, with my father bellowing instructions as we loaded the boat. If we had the guns, we forgot the ammunition, if we had the ammunition, we forgot the dogs. I said I would rather be a Communist than go through all this again in full view of hundreds of Chinese, hysterical with laughter. This remark drove my father quite insane. The fact was that, ammunition or no ammunition, none of us knew how to use the guns anyway. The Portuguese Navy would not have been much use, because they spent all their time with their ships moored to the jetty, doing their laundry, which then festooned the rigging. Any attempt on their part to stop the Red Peril descending upon the British Consulate, raping, burning, looting and desecrating the picture of Her Majesty The Queen, would be bound to end miserably in a hail of Portuguese bullets, fired from under the bedclothes.

At the end of the summer holidays, my sister and brother returned to England, my sister to train as an occupational therapist, and my brother to go back to school. During the holidays, my mother had tried to invite the bright young things from Hong Kong to come and stay, but nearly everyone had heard about my father; the few that had not, arrived for the weekend and left after twenty-four hours of his company. My poor sister had had months of this before

I arrived, and had endured ghastly social embarrassment as my mother tried to find a suitable boyfriend with the right sort of connections, and my father frightened them off. No wonder she had looked so thin and ill.

I decided to get away from it all, and applied for a job in Hong Kong as a secretary in a small Foreign Office department. The interview took place in a big secretariat, amongst potted plants and people bent over desks, writing furiously. The man in charge was very nice, and knew my mother who had pulled all sorts of strings to get me this job. She had raked over a posse of titled elderly friends, who all wrote references saying I was 'honest and reliable' and 'trustworthy and loyal'. I did not know any of them and they did not know me, otherwise they would never have written anything so foolish. I got the job, and my mother booked me into the Helena May Club for young ladies, otherwise known as the 'Virgins' Retreat'.

My job turned out to be highly secret. My first duty of the day was to arrive at eight o'clock, open the door in a special way, and then turn off an alarm system which wired up the whole office to the police station. The cleaners would then come in and I had to watch that they did not cast spying eyes on any information we had. They were not to take anything from the waste-paper baskets, because every day I was driven by car, clutching the contents of all those baskets, to the secretariat where it would all be burned. However, the 'Yellow Peril' was everywhere and I had to supervise.

The staff were nice, well-meaning people, who took their jobs very seriously. Our telephone switchboard had four numbers: two legitimate ones for the business we pretended to be in; two secret ones for agents. All over Hong Kong there were little businesses operating as travel agents, or import–export agents, which were really a cloak for the deadliest, most secret operations of British Intelligence. Of course, all over Hong Kong, there were other travel agents or import–export firms, American, Dutch, German, etc., all cloaking the deadliest, most secret operations of their respective Intelligences. So that, when one little Red Chinaman got to Hong Kong, heaving a huge sigh of relief, he found his fortune was made overnight, recounting his story to agents of all nationalities. Peter, who was in charge of our agents, could be seen lurking down by the docks, collecting information. One day an agent gave him a Chinese sweetmeat, and he returned to the office, pale and green, utterly convinced that he had been poisoned by the other side. He faced death bravely, was sick on the carpet, and then recovered.

I found my job terribly tedious, because I was the dogsbody. I had to cut out of the papers all the articles from mainland China and stick them in a book. I also had to answer the telephone; because the legitimate lines were always busy, I gave the secret numbers to my boyfriends so they could get through to me quickly, and Peter would often find himself using code words to some second-lieutenant. When I had to carry letters to our other office, I usually did a little shopping on the way, and once I lost a whole batch of letters in a department store. My boss behaved as though I had given away details of the Second Coming. I had a feeling that the job would not last long, I think not so much because of my ineptitude as my inability to take the situation seriously. As Hong Kong had a fairly small social circle, the staff all tended to meet at dinner parties, and when someone there asked me what I did, I found that by clamping my lips tightly together, lowering my eyes, and saying nobly, 'I cannot possibly tell you,' I gained the individual attention of the whole table—much to the fury of my colleagues, who were unable to stop me, as we were not supposed to recognize each other outside the office.

My mother had been having trouble with her back, and was not well. She went into hospital in Hong Kong with a slipped disc, and I had to take over her duties as hostess. Unfortunately, it was just about then that I discovered men and alcohol, more or less simultaneously, so I was a little erratic. I was just seventeen, and would like to have been described as mysterious and sophisticated, but with a few drinks in me I tended to become more like an ebullient puppy. Still, I had to be tolerated, because I was taking my mother's place at dinner parties in Macao, and representing both my parents at social functions in Hong Kong, as my father rarely left his base.

The first time I accepted a formal invitation on behalf of my parents, I went to the hospital to consult my mother. She gave me lots of advice on how to behave, and made me promise to return home by midnight, because 'nice girls' always went home before twelve, leaving the other sort to do questionable things under the table. I promised, and went to buy a dress. My mother had said it had to be long, so I bought the most beautiful dress with yards and yards of skirt, more of a ball dress actually. I got so carried away with my appearance that I bought a pair of long white gloves that went right up to my elbows with small pearl buttons at the wrist.

The day came, and I spent hours soaking in a hot bath and getting ready. The taxi deposited me on the doorstep of a very imposing house. The hostess was very kind, and the other guests made me welcome. None of the other women was wearing anything approaching my outfit, but I did not mind, even though when I sat down at the dinner table my skirt cascaded over the laps of the gentlemen sitting on either side of me. I decided that I could not eat with the gloves on, and I worked out that by unbuttoning the slit in the wrists I could free my hands sufficiently to eat. However the loose fingers flopped into my food and I resolved to ask my mother about such niceties. During the meal, I thought I was being witty and fascinating, and then I remember nothing more. I woke up the next morning in my hostess's nightdress. She was a little frigid at breakfast, hinting that I had had too much to drink. I told her that I had been working too hard, but I could see she did not believe me. The word got round that I was trouble and the matrons of the colony worried about the effect I would have on their daughters.

The subject of virginity occupied my mind almost constantly. There were two schools of thought at Helena May: the advisability of 'keeping it for the right man' was the one that prevailed. Not only did the man in question have to be socially acceptable, but also financially sound. Waiting to exchange virginity for matrimony did not, however, preclude endless discussions of sex among our 'set' or lots of heavy petting with the young Naval officers and businessmen on the island. I found the young men in Hong Kong very like the callow youths of my early days at St Mary's. Most of them had fast cars, roaming hands, and an ability to hold their drink. It was all very unsatisfactory and repetitious and I was eager and curious to find out more.

It seemed useless to pursue my enquiries among the British on the island, so I looked around for and found some very exciting older men. One of them, Ivor, who worked with the Norwegian Shipping Line, seemed an excellent choice, as he had his own house, and a speedboat. The girls who went out with his friends were decidedly 'common' by my mother's standards, but they were refreshingly straightforward and had obviously 'done it' by the casual way they retired with their lovers after dinner to various bedrooms in Ivor's house. After a few evenings of strenuous skirmishes in Ivor's dining room, I decided that the moment had come to give up my virginity in the cause of experience—which would make me the most interesting member of my group at the Helena May Club.

Accordingly I dressed with care, removing the safety pins from my bra straps, and dousing myself liberally with 'Miss Dior'. After a romantic dinner, Ivor suggested that we repair to his bedroom, and I eagerly galloped after him. However, I came to a skidding halt when I suddenly remembered that, despite my interesting time in London with the Air Force officer, Joe, I had never undressed before a man. Come to that, I had never undressed before another human being, not even my sister. Shades of the Reverend Mother blew across the room. Taking a deep breath, I ordered Ivor out of the room. 'Okay,' he said amiably.

Panic set in, I checked under his pillow for his pyjamas, and found some there, to my relief. I put them on, but the pyjama trousers were far too tight, and they welded my legs indissolubly together. By hopping vigorously towards the bed I managed to heave myself horizontally into a prone position and then to pull the sheet right up to my nose. Ivor knocked on the door, and after taking a deep breath, I said, 'Come in,' in what I hoped was a seductive whisper, miserably aware that it emerged as a high-pitched squeak of alarm. He entered naked except for a towel wrapped around his waist. Great gusts of 'Old Spice' wafted across the room. 'Darling', he said, and dropped his towel. . . .

The only human male anatomy available for my inspection up to then had been statues, heavily shrouded in vine leaves. I had never seen a naked man before, and certainly not a naked man with an erection. As Ivor advanced towards me, I let out a loud shriek and pointing dramatically between his legs, I said, in my best convent voice, 'You are not going to put that inside me.' Nonplussed, he stood still. I pulled the sheet over my head, and then in a huge leap, to the sound of rending pyjamas, I left the bed, gathered my clothes in one hand, and rushed into the bathroom. It took me sixty seconds to get dressed and crash out of the front door, and away down the road. I could hear Ivor calling me plaintively but I kept running. Near the hostel, I slowed down. Sauntering through the main door and upstairs, I met several girls to whom I had boasted that tonight was to be the night. They all looked at me expectantly. 'What was it like?' asked one of my closest allies. 'Not all it's cracked up to be,' I said nonchalantly, and sauntered into my room. I decided to put the whole matter of virginity on ice for the next few years, or maybe the rest of my life.

When my mother went back to Macao from the hospital, she was wearing a plastic jacket for her back, and seemed still to be in great pain. Nevertheless she organized from her bed the official cocktail party to launch the Grand Prix, and I posted the usual invitations to the matrons who ran Hong Kong society. I carefully left out six of the women I most disliked, and when they arrived at our door, purring sweetly, to say that I must have forgotten their invitations, I took pleasure in saying that indeed I had not forgotten and that it was simply that I did not want them in the house. The diplomatic repercussions went on for weeks, but I did not notice, because my mother had to go back into hospital.

The last memory I have of her in Macao was when Chung, the lecherous dressmaker, came to measure me for a suit. Sally, our dachshund, was beside me watching him measure my chest. My mother was lying on her bed giving advice. Chung's hand strayed, and Sally, who was as vigilant as Mother when it came to sex, leapt upon him and removed a large piece of cloth from his behind. Chung, enraged, jumped high in the air. My mother laughed loudly. It was the last time I heard her laugh. The hospital told my father that she had secondary growths in the spine and that she must return to England for treatment. She decided to fly home to 'Hunthay'. My father was to clear up his affairs, and then we would join her.

NINE

England: The Last Act

WHEN MY MOTHER had gone on the plane back to England my father was distraught, and cried all the time; much as he abused her, she was his whole world. He kept telling me how the doctor had said 'Your wife *was* a fine woman', from which he had known that she was going to die. One of her close friends, who was the Ambassador in Japan, sent my father a new experimental drug which was thought to have some effect on her disease but had not yet been tested. Because it was illegal for the drug to be distributed before the tests were run, my father had to travel on the same plane with it back to England. I chose to follow by boat with the baggage, and part of me prayed that my mother would be dead before I got back.

My father left on a BOAC plane in the early hours of the morning. When it came down to land in Karachi, it had engine trouble and all the passengers were transferred to another plane, except my father who had to remain with the drug which could only be taken off that particular plane in England. The relief plane crashed, killing everyone. Mother heard that he was dead, but of course he was not. It took me six weeks to get home by boat, and by the time I reached our house in Devon my father had lost any self-control he had ever had.

'Hunthay' looked just the same as it always had. The love and care that my mother had put into the house had paid off. The sitting room, the square hall and the comfortable kitchen smelt of furniture polish and glowed with blues and greens from the Chinese bowls, filled with rose petals from the garden. The Chinese carpets lay shimmering in muted shades of ochre and brown, and outside, the whole of the front of the house was festooned with climbing roses. I put my suitcase in the hall, and kissed my sister who looked white and strained. She introduced me to the housekeeper who had been employed by my mother to look after us. It was obvious that within a few minutes of his arrival my father had taken a dislike to her, and that it was mutual. But Mrs Jones loved my mother very much. She was an elderly widow, forced to take housekeeping jobs to get by financially. She had an old Springer spaniel who was the one remaining link with her husband, whom she had adored. Her standards were those of the old-fashioned, upright middle class, and my father offended everything she believed in, but it was to her credit that, instead of responding to his insulting behaviour, she realized that it must be unendurable for us, and did not leave us, but stayed beside us to the bitter end. Her code of honour did not allow her to discuss his behaviour with us, but she was always there, a rock and an anchor.

I arrived in time to see my mother that afternoon in hospital. I was dreadfully shocked at the change in her. She was no longer the pretty young woman with vibrant blue eyes and glossy chestnut hair. The disease had washed the colour from her eyes and her beautiful long hair lay in greying hanks around her face. I kissed her and I could smell the fear and pain that imprisoned her. I put my strong young arms around her, wishing frantically that I could pour part of my warm and living self into her racked body to help her to get well again. She looked at me with such longing, and smiled at me through cracked lips, saying that she was glad I was home. I felt dreadfully guilty for having wished she would die before I reached her. I could see now that the end would be long in coming, and that she would need me.

My father sat on the end of the bed and began to berate her because she had asked for peaches, which were out of season. His voice choked and shook with anger as he informed us of the price of such fruit. He put out his hands and said, 'Look how they're shaking. I'm having a breakdown. Nobody cares.' He went on to enumerate his ailments, his sleeplessness, his lack of appetite, and then he asked my sister and me to leave the room. We stood outside in the corridor. My sister told me that my father spent most of his time during visiting hours simply tormenting our mother, because he was determined to make her sign a legal document making it possible for him to withdraw the money that they had tucked away in Canada. She was steadfastly refusing to sign, partly because she did not want to believe that she was going to die, but also because she realized that if she did then we would be totally at his mercy. We could hear his voice rising and falling, and then her low, muffled sobbing. I called the nurses, who were at the end of the corridor, and begged them to stop it. They looked at us sympathetically, but said there was nothing they could do. They could not interfere between man and wife.

I went back into the room where my mother lay quiet now, and exhausted. My father sat on the chair, his eyes flashing with anger. 'It's time to go home,' I said, and I kissed her goodbye. On the way home in the car he grumbled and groaned. I realized that he could feel no pain for her or for anyone but himself. Life had betrayed him once again, and he was lashing out against it like a wounded animal.

Every day for months we visited her in hospital. While we were in the house, there was a terrible silence, broken only by his monologue of self-pity. We did only what he allowed us to do. In the evenings we sat watching his television programmes, and I would accompany him on long walks through the countryside. He had frequent outbursts of rage when he would insult Mrs Jones or scream at my sister, who was growing still thinner and quieter. Because I knew him better, I could quiet him more easily. He was more wary of me, though it was my sister who would retaliate when pushed beyond endurance. I never raised my voice, and was somehow able to handle him. No one came to visit us—the friends that my mother had kept would visit her in hospital, but stayed away from us, because they were afraid of this huge, brooding man. The more frightened he became, the more he needed absolute control over the household, so that we were constantly at his beck and call, and would only leave the house to visit the hospital.

On good days my mother would sit in a wheelchair in the hospital grounds, so that she could see the roof of the house she loved so much. She begged my father to let her go home, with a trained nurse, but he refused because he said he could not afford it. So she lay imprisoned in the little hospital. The drug from Japan had failed to halt the invading cancer and all treatment had been stopped. Her left arm had swollen enormously. The pain at times was so intense that her whole body would be convulsed. She would groan and cry out. The nurses tried to make me leave the room, but I knew that she needed me there close to her, and I would sit beside her, holding her hand, and sing 'Summer Time' until she lay quiet again. Then I would kiss her, and go home—to him. As I listened to him rambling on about the past, I sensed his desperation and helplessness, and tried to comfort him by holding his hand.

The day came when the doctor told my father there was nothing more they could do for my mother. She was taking up a bed needed for the living and she must be moved. I begged him to bring her home, but he was adamant. He insisted he could not afford the fees for a private nurse, and he arranged to have her moved to a home for incurables, which worked out cheaper. She hated the indignity of this, and a few days before she was due to go to the home, they had a particularly violent session, with my father screaming at her to sign over the money. I begged her to sign the document, so that he would at last give her some peace. I explained that I would always care for my brother and sister, and that the money was immaterial. She reluctantly agreed and Mrs Jones and a friend witnessed her signature, while he guided her crippled hand over the paper. She wept through the whole proceedings, and when we were driving home, my father exploded at me, accusing me of wanting the money, and encouraging her to hold out against him. Once inside the house, he went to his desk and feverishly did his sums and countless lists. The money was now his, but still he did not find the peace I had hoped the triumph might grant him.

The ambulance to take her to the home arrived at the hospital at nine in the morning, and I saw the look on her face. She had at last resigned herself to dying. On the way to the home, we stopped on a hill, and my mother looked down for the last time at 'Hunthay' in the distance. I think that the house was the only thing she had ever loved, and the bitterness of not being able to die there broke her heart. The home was like a great many nursing homes, clean and efficient, but so impersonal. She had a private room with French windows on to the garden. The rose beds were just outside. The lawns were velvet green, and the last few weeks of her life were spent gazing at the roses, and they, at least, served to remind her of 'Hunthay'.

My father decided that my brother must leave school to be with us. I argued against it, feeling that my father was so unstable that my brother would be safer away from it all. Also the drugs my mother had been given deepened her voice to that of a man, and long whiskers grew from her chin. The disease had distorted her limbs so that she was unrecognizable: I did not want my brother to see her. But my father was unshakeable in his wish. I set off for the school determined to persuade the headmaster to refuse to let my brother go. The headmaster was quite unsympathetic and when I described my father's behaviour he would not believe me and said that I was hysterical. I took my brother home.

My mother was taking great comfort from God. She would talk for long periods of time to an angel at the foot of her bed, and say to it that it was not yet time to leave. Sometimes she would mistake me for a long-dead friend, and talk to me about things that had happened when she was young. Then her face would light up and her eyes would suddenly come alive, and she would look sixteen again, and hold my hand and say how nice it was that I had come to see her after so long. Sometimes she was bitter against my father and regretted the life they had had together. I asked her why she had not left him. 'I stayed for your sakes,' she said, '. . . for your schooling and your futures.' And I thought how wonderful it would have been to have lived away from him all those years. What good had all that fear done? Now she was leaving us to him.

On the last day, we arrived as usual at about eleven o'clock. My brother, who was not yet thirteen, found the hours by her bedside quite intolerable, so he would roam the gardens. I knew that morning when I saw her, that it was the end. She was barely conscious, but she did beg me to look after my sister and brother, and then she said that she loved my father and asked me to look after him too. She then lapsed back into unconsciousness. The fluid had built up in her stomach to such an extent that she was constantly restless and uncomfortable. She woke again briefly and asked me to sing 'There is a green hill far away,' and then she asked for it to be sung at her funeral. My father came in and said that he was hungry and it was time for lunch at home. I asked if I could stay and explained I was afraid that she might die all alone, but he refused and I was too fearful of him to insist.

We drove along the winding Devon roads, and as we were sitting down at the table the phone rang. 'Your mother has passed away,' said the matron, and I felt a sense of utter desolation as I had failed to be with her. She had died alone in that room with no one there to comfort her. I went into the dining room and told my father. I had to lower my eyes in case he should see the hatred I felt for him at that moment. But he was too absorbed in his own pain. Tears gushed down his cheeks and caught in the creases in his jowls. We sat politely around the table waiting for him to stop. When he did we went back in the car to the nursing home.

The French windows were shut, and we went into her room through the inside door. The room was darkened. She lay remote and silent, no longer twisting and whimpering. Her face looked slightly disdainful, and her hair was neatly plaited. 'Kiss your mother,' said my father. None of us wanted to go near the corpse. We were very afraid, but we were more afraid of him, so we bent over her and each in turn kissed her.

We were just leaving the gates of the home. I was sitting in the front seat of the car with my father, who was sobbing, when suddenly I felt an enormous surge of loving warmth. It was a feeling of peace, and the sure knowledge that she was eternal made me smile hugely, and I turned to my sister to see her too grinning from ear to ear. I knew from that moment onward that we all belong to God, and that my mother had not suffered in vain. All the way home I comforted myself with the phrase, 'The peace of God that passeth all understanding.'

When we got home my father told Mrs Jones to leave, but she insisted he give her a month's notice. She must have had some premonition of what was to come. The next day my father said that my mother's body was coming home. I had no idea what happened to a body when death occurred in a household, so I just accepted the news that she would be with us for a day or two. However, when the undertaker came with the coffin, the lid had not been screwed down. It made me feel uneasy. My father made us clear the dining room and put the table and the chairs in the hall. The undertaker set up trestles and put the coffin on them. He advised me to keep the windows open, as it was a hot September. I did not know why he said that, and he did not tell me. He left, shaking us all by the hand.

My father spent the rest of the day in the room. We could hear him sobbing and ranting and then just as it was getting dark he called us in. He had lit the candles in their silver candelabra and they flamed softly, throwing a mellow light on the highly polished coffin with its brass handles. The coffin was covered with a purple pall, and as we stood in the doorway my father said that we were to come in and say a prayer for my mother. We stood round the coffin, and I said that I did not want to look at her, and that he was not to remove the purple pall or we would leave the room. He agreed. We bent our heads and closed our eyes, and prayed silently, and when I opened my eyes I saw that he had pulled the pall away and we were gazing at her. Her face had changed overnight. The bridge of her nose had gone blue, and her nostrils had been stuffed with cottonwool. The three of us stood transfixed, and I began to shout at him. He retaliated with a long screaming row about how I wanted to throw my mother's body on a rubbish heap, and he followed me around the house, pouring out his love and hatred. I calmed down and realized that he was now really out of his mind and that the best thing to do was for me to remain calm and then get help.

We sat down to dinner outside in the hall. We did not feel like eating, but my father grew angry, so we ate. He gorged as usual and went on with his monologue at the head of the table. As soon as the meal was over, we went for a walk. I took my brother back into the room and knelt beside him and explained that his father was beside himself with grief. I did not believe that the child understood, but there was peace in that room then.

We went to bed as soon as the washing-up was done. My father remained downstairs, roaming round the coffin and crying and mumbling. We lay upstairs afraid of what he would do next. Would he take the body out? During the night I crept to her room and there on the floor, in a shaft of moonlight, was a pair of her tiny AA shoes. They looked so abandoned lying there. I missed her fiercely. Then I went back to bed.

The second day came and then the third and then the fourth. Nothing changed except the smell, and it started seeping out from the room. My father, in order to keep up his emotional frenzy, arranged games to terrorize us. He sent my sister upstairs to fetch a pair of scissors. When she came down to the hall, he had pulled my mother's plaits over the edge of the coffin and rested both her hands on the edges. My sister screamed loudly. I ran into the room. 'I only wanted to take a lock of her hair,' he said innocently. I looked at her beloved face, which was now grotesquely different from the one I had known. The cheeks had fallen in, and the lips were drawn back. I begged him to bury her, but he refused.

On this fourth day he called our family doctor to come in and make sure that she was dead. I felt some hope that the doctor, who had been a great friend of my mother, would force him to bury her. The doctor came, went into the room, stayed ten minutes and then walked out of the house. The only comment he made to Mrs Jones was that 'It shouldn't happen to a dog'.

I went to the vicar but he would not interfere. I tried our next-door neighbours. They gave me a cup of tea and sympathy, but they would not interfere. Everyone knew what was happening: three children, a corpse, and a man, mad with grief. But no one did anything.

Finally he buried her, and we stood by her graveside, looking down at the small coffin. She was finally gone.

Epilogue

MY MOTHER AND Christopher both died agonizing and undig-
nified deaths. Why? I still don't know. I do realize that what happened to my mother created a need in me to give shelter to women
and children, and that gradually as I saw more and more men like
my father my anger turned to compassion. One way of looking at
my father's value as a human being is that as a result of his behaviour there is now refuge, not only in England but across the
world: therefore his life was valuable. Also, the understanding that
comes to children in the family circle will be re-enacted through
generations to come. So what began as a destructive course in my
life was changed into something creative and good.

As far as Christopher is concerned, his influence on my life
was enormous, which is why this book exists and also why it is
dedicated to him. I suppose the reasons for living and dying are
something I shall continue to question all my life. It seems to me
that all human beings are on an eternal journey. Everyone has his
own path to follow and the question is always 'Who am I?' When
we find out we need no longer ask. So much of what I have
learned has been from the mothers and children that come through
the refuge. But the place I am always happiest in is the Bristol
house.

Since I wrote the Prologue to this book, about Christopher,
two years have elapsed. I still visit Bristol though not nearly so
regularly. Carmen, our administrator, has taken over the weekly
visit and I just go when I can or when I am overwhelmed by the
misery and struggle at the Chiswick refuge and need to reassure
myself that people do change and violent children can settle. I get
into the car and hurtle down the M4 to the 'big house', as it is
called by those who have moved out, and then having said hello

there I go off and visit the others who have moved into their own homes around Bristol.

I usually go straight to Maureen's, where I get a huge welcome from my two dogs Sam and Bess. They are Staffordshire bull terriers and Maureen took them on from me because I felt I was beginning to neglect them as the problems of work got greater. She loves all animals and they have been with her for two years now and are completely happy. When I walk in they will go berserk for a while but then settle down, usually in the best chairs while I perch on a hard dining chair. Sam does look at me rather guiltily, but it's 'dogs' rule OK' at Maureen's so he doesn't move. Mark, her son, is huge now—much taller than I am—and is no more aggressive than any other boy of his age. He still has trouble with male teachers who are aggressive towards him but I am confident that he will not grow up to be a violent adult. Kim, his sister, has a gentle loving boyfriend which is again a good sign, as the usual pattern is that girls from violent families are attracted to violent boys.

Maureen is always the same, usually broke but always beaming. She has learned to be so much less aggressive and so articulate that she can even out-argue me. We have travelled together to lecture— the first time when I was invited to Holland to talk to groups there, and I hired three camping vans and took nineteen mothers and children to Amsterdam, Bonn, Brussels and then Paris, and later to Berlin and to attend the Frankfurt Book Fair. Every time I settle down in her little house we start, 'Do you remember . . .' and off we go. I think she finds it amazing that for sixteen years she was a battered wife and now she is the first battered wife to have given evidence to Parliament, and that she has travelled, made a film with me that has been shown in many parts of the world and, above all, made a new life for herself.

After chatting to Maureen I go over to see Jeannie whose family was one of those that passed through the 'big house'. She has six kids and they all came on the Amsterdam trip. Jeannie is lovely and warm and the children are very special because at one point in the 'big house' Jeannie fell in love with a man who was violent and took off with him with all the children. I was distraught, but as it happened she had completed the time necessary to qualify for a house and the letter arrived at the 'big house'. A woman phoned me to say her new house was ready and waiting. All I could think of doing was to contact her old social worker because we had heard a rumour that Jeannie had gone back to her old estate. Sure enough she was there. I asked her to phone me which she did. 'You've got a house,' I said. 'Do you want it?' . . . 'Yes,' she said and we both heaved a sigh of relief.

Jeannie was back and installed within a matter of a few days. Apart from having learned of the danger of jumping into an immediate relationship, Jeannie also, I realized, needed to create a situation where she could go back to the estate where she had lived for years, not only to see her friends but also to see her husband. Violent and terrible as he had been, they had shared six children and many years of marriage. He was her first and only man during all those years and she needed to check that what she had now was preferable to what she had left behind. She told me that when he heard that she was back on the estate, in homeless family accommodation, and he turned up as she knew he would, she was amazed to find that she did not feel anything at all. It was like talking to a stranger, but most important of all, she was no longer afraid of him. That was the most significant thing in that whole experience. The ties were finally broken. The children saw him but didn't feel they wanted to see him again, so what started out as a disaster turned out to be a beneficial experience. Now they live on an estate near Maureen and they have as many animals as humans in the house. They all argue among themselves but stick together like glue.

A final visit is usually to Eileen, Christopher's mum, who has made a palace out of her maisonette. Both girls are doing well. Phil is still diabetic but will get to University because she is a real bluestocking, while Margaret, though not as academic as her sister, will probably go into one of the caring professions. Eileen always fusses round when I go there and I get quantities of tea. She still misses her older son but I'm pleased she has coped so well and not made her loss a burden for the girls.

I hear news of Pat and Bob. The last time they came to the 'big house' it was to show us their little baby girl. Daniel and Jason were incredibly proud of her and then they rushed off into the garden to play with the others. It wasn't long before Dan fell over as usual and came howling into the sitting room. 'Come here, son,' said Bob, and Dan went straight into his arms. I got a lump in my throat and wondered why life seems to have been edited by *Reader's Digest*.

Peter pops into the 'big house' occasionally. The mothers see Noela and say how marvellous she looks. She has gone back to nursing and before she moved out she and I both agreed that Peter would do best in a boarding school. He is unusually bright and needs stretching or he is miserable and unhappy. Noela put him into child guidance and they agreed and got him a place near us with very kindly monks. I was very worried about it to begin with, remembering my own unfortunate experience in the convent, but after our first visit to see Peter I realized I had nothing to worry about. Peter was fine. He should do very well.

Not all the families have been a success story. I can think of one mother who moved out who really worries me. She wasn't cruel to the children, she just neglected them. Fortunately, they were old enough to look after themselves but they needed the love from the other mothers in the community. However, there was no way she was going to change or ever co-operate and she left as soon as possible. It is always sad when you lose a mother, but maybe the children will have seen a glimpse of what a loving, sharing life can be like and that will be enough to sustain them till they are free to make their own choices. I hope so.

As I drive away from the 'big house', having kissed all the children goodbye, and swing round the roundabout at Frenchey and come up on to the M4 on the long drive back to London, I feel I have created another St Mary's only better, because the children have their mothers with them. One day we may be able to offer second-stage houses to single-parent fathers as well as mothers. There are many men struggling to look after their children having been abandoned by unscrupulous wives, and children also need fathers.

One reason why what has happened in Bristol is so satisfying to me is that I still believe there is no such thing as an expert. There are people who know a great deal about a certain subject and it is as well to consult them if you need that particular piece of advice, but it does not mean that they are then well qualified to be an expert in all fields. Usually the best expert is one's own experience, with an ear to the inner voice that we all have. In women it is dismissed as mere 'intuition', and as it is considered a womanly quality, it is educated out of men. But it is there in us all and everyone will know the feeling of pure certainty that can follow a period of doubt and indecision. During the whole history of Chiswick Women's Aid I have always followed my own inner voice. Sometimes it has brought me into direct conflict with the authorities, but provided I follow it calmly, things have so far always turned out well for the refuge.

In 1971 I was running a little house with four rooms and an outside lavatory. A small group of local women were working with me and together we offered advice, play-group facilities, and a meeting place for isolated mothers with young children in our community. One day a middle-aged woman came in, and asked me to help her. She was very hesitant, but finally she took off her jumper and showed me purple bruises which extended over her breasts down to her waist. Her husband had beaten her with a chair leg. She had gone to the social services and they had told her to go home. 'No one will help me,' she said. Those words threw me back fourteen years. I could hear once again my own voice begging for help, and I could not believe that, after all these years, nothing had changed at all. Women were still forced to live with intolerable men, because no one would help them. I put my arm around her and said, 'Of course I will help you. You can stay here.'

That was our first mother, and soon she was followed by thousands of other women, bringing their children. Chiswick Women's Aid, a refuge for battered wives, was born. It was the first refuge of its kind in the world, and to it the most dedicated and caring people came. They have worked for very little money, and then for nothing when the money ran out. Soon other groups started up, and the National Federation of Women's Aid gathered many groups under its umbrella. We are not members, because we have always remained apolitical, and the Federation held clear views on the position of women in society. We admire them and their work and co-operate with them wherever possible. In the last three years refuges have opened up in Holland, Germany, Australia, Canada, New Zealand and America.

I visited the Dutch refuge when it first opened. They had a

beautiful house, and very caring staff, who faced the same problems that we did, the major one being the indifference of the government to what is essentially a national problem. The same is not true in Berlin, for the government there sent observers to Chiswick, and then invited me over to show our film and discuss the setting up of refuges with the Berlin group of women. They also gave a generous sum of money to the group to enable them to employ staff to care for the mothers and children. The same intelligent appreciation of the problem cannot be said to be true of France, Italy and Spain. There, the governments turn a blind eye, not only to violence towards women and children, but also towards all conditions affecting the lives of women in those countries, such as abortion, divorce, work opportunities, support for the unmarried mother and her children. But it will not last forever, for the wind of liberation has blown across the world, and whereas the suffragettes fought for tangible goals, such as the vote, all women are now demanding the right to their own bodies, to make their own decisions, and to free themselves from bad relationships without fear of sanctions from a punitive church or society.

The situation is much brighter in America and Canada. I spent three weeks on the Eastern seaboard of the United States, travelling through sixteen cities in that time. Everywhere we found great enthusiasm and understanding of the problem. A lunch was given in our honour at the House of Representatives, which seemed incredibly ironic to me, as all they do in England is keep taking me to court for overcrowding! The room was full of interested Congressmen, which made me reflect on the first occasion that the M.P. Jack Ashley brought up the matter of battered wives in the House of Commons. There was nobody in the chamber except himself and the answering Minister. As Jack said, if he had been talking about dogs the place would have been packed.

The one note of criticism I have of all the countries that are bravely struggling to open refuge, is that I do not believe the problem of violence in the family belongs to the women's movement alone. I cannot see how you can call for the liberation of one sex without liberating the other. It has always been vital for us to employ good and gentle men to work in Chiswick with the women and children. Many of the mothers have never known a kind and non-violent man, and Michael Dunn, who works at the refuge, is their first experience of a man who can be sympathetic, helpful, sexually non-aggressive; to many women who arrive there it is a revelation. The same is true for the children. They often flinch away from the play-group leaders, but when they see Mike Taylor and Roger Blades bathing and changing a baby, or feeding a toddler, they watch fascinated. They see Steve Topple carrying around a crying child and cuddling it, and they soon join in. This is the vital beginning—to learn that not all men are brutal and explosive and that copying the play-group leaders leads on to happy experiences. Therefore those groups that seek to exclude men from working within the refuge are doing the mothers and children a great disservice. It is one thing to be going through a personal crisis and discovering your own identity as a woman, which may mean rejecting male society for a time—a perfectly healthy step in female liberation—but to protect what is a personal need as a political doctrine is dangerous, and the groups which do this do not have our support. Certainly much of the credit for the work done both in England and abroad must go to feminists who have fought so hard to bring this problem to the attention of the public and governments, but, at the end of the day, to say that women are beaten because we live in a patriarchal and male-dominated society is nonsense, because women and children are beaten in Russia where they have a serious problem of wife abuse, and in China. The interesting thing about China is that the offending partner, be it male or female, has to account for his act of violence immediately to his local commune leaders. This approach seems far more practical than the punitive attempts to legislate in courts against human behaviour. One day, I hope to go back to China and see if they are any nearer to solving the problem than we are.

I have never hated any of the men who have come to the refuge for their wives. Some have brutally assaulted their wives and children. Some have even killed, but when you enter their reality and feel the intense suffering that drove them to commit their violent and outraged actions, you can only feel compassion for them. Mr Jones killed his two-year-old stepdaughter in a fit of rage. He put her body in a suitcase and carefully and lovingly put in her favourite toys around her before leaving her on a golf course. He has never forgiven himself, but he could not cope with a busy toddler, and he lashed out too hard. Mr White stood with an old newspaper clipping in his hand. It was a description of how his stepfather, who had been violent towards his family all his life, had cut his throat in front of the family when Mr White was thirteen. Now he was beating his wife. 'Why?' he kept asking, 'Why am I doing what he did to us?' 'Echoes of your childhood,' I said, and we talked for hours.

I believe that the roots of violence lie in bad parenting. The damage is handed down from generation to generation, gradually spreading and affecting the society we live in. England for a long time has been relatively stable and a non-violent community, but we must remember that two world wars got rid of a lot of our violent men, and until relatively recently, we exported our troublesome men to Australia, South Africa, New Zealand, Rhodesia and other parts of the Empire. 'Go west, young man,' we said, shoving boatloads of youngsters from Barnardo's on to far-flung farms in Canada. When they became independent, these countries decided they would no longer allow British human rejects to enter, so we are stuck with our problems on our doorstep. The figures for violent crimes rise steadily every year. The prisons are grossly overcrowded and the staff work on with the hopeless knowledge that persistent violent offenders will return again and again.

For a long time alcoholics were seen as criminals and punished severely. A while ago it began to be realized that they were ill, and accordingly treated with care and compassion. I feel the same about violent offenders. Violence is caused by a disordered personality. Custodial care is often necessary with a violent offender, but useless unless treatment is offered at the same time. By 'treatment' I mean a programme of re-socializing—a chance to learn again all the lessons that most people have learned in years of family life. Those of us who have never shared those experiences are like strangers at the feast. We are constantly puzzled by how the world relates to each of us. We are 'outsiders'. It is necessary to give us another chance. It is easy to lock up a body and force it to perform endless duties to order, but unless you can touch the spirit, you will achieve nothing. We need lots of theraputic communities all over England to replace the prisons which we all know do little to alter human behaviour.

If you accept that it is the mother and father who have almost total control over a young child until the age of five, when they branch out and go to school, you must also acknowledge the amount of harm that bad parents can do in that time. After all the Jesuits have always said, 'Give me the boy until the age of seven, and I will give you a man.' Because we all want to believe that the family is a loving and warm and secure unit, we tend to resist any evidence that proves the contrary. There is also the chilling thought that if people are allowed to poke their noses into other people's family life, who knows what skeletons would fall out of the family cupboards? After all, most of us have lashed out at our partners and children at some time and the parenting of children is the most complicated and delicate task undertaken by human beings. A pediatrician takes several years studying child care. Parents are supposed to know by some sort of divine guidance just exactly what to do. So most parents spend their lives in a permanent miasma of guilt and when they see a picture of a bruised face of a small toddler they tend to think 'There but for the grace of God go I'. All these discussions about caring for children, home-making and marital relationships are very threatening, because none of us can live up to the ideal set out in books, magazines and on television, and so again we fail in our own eyes.

Surely education is one of the major steps towards better human relationships. It is so vital to teach the study of human relationships as a subject in school. It always amazes me that schools are quite willing to spend hours teaching children about the plumbing aspects of sex and reproduction, but nothing at all about the responsibilities that go with it. Also, apart from the parents the most significant factor in a child's life is school and teachers. If teachers are trained to think that what happens to a child at home is none of their business, what chance has a troubled child to ask for help, except to act out its disruptive and dangerous ways which will merely result in punishment. The teacher in this case is the one who should be punished, because by imposing a barrier between a child's experiences at home and at school he forces the child to communicate his misery and fear in the only way he can: by acting out symbolically the roles of the parents who are in conflict. If it is the father who is violent, the boys will be violent and aggressive and most of the girls withdrawn and silent. However, if the mother beats the girls they will be as dangerous as the boys. Punishing them is a waste of time. Nothing a school can do to these children can efface the punishments they have had at home. The only remedy is to remove them to a separate unit, where they can be with adults they can trust. This way, over a period of time, controls can be built up which will enable them to cope well enough to go back to school.

Children's houses should be established where children who feel they cannot tolerate their parents' behaviour can go to live as an alternative community. In many cases they may choose to move freely between their community home and their parents, but children should have the right to choose where they live, and not be condemned to a life of misery because they are the possessions of two people. As the poet Kahlil Gibran has said:

> Your children are not your children
> They are the sons and daughters of Life's longing for itself.
> They come through you, but not from you,
> And though they are with you yet they belong not to you.

So much of the anger that is locked away in children, to erupt into violence in later years, is occasioned not merely by the awful treatment of some parents but also by resentment at the rest of a world that has allowed the child to be trapped inside this lonely prison. It is possible to teach a child, from about nine years old onwards, some degree of compassion towards the behaviour of its parents. This lessens the rage and pain within the child, but it has to be done when such children are safe from attack, as indeed they are with us at the refuge. There is a ridiculous disposition on the part of many adults to pretend that all parents are godlike, and therefore never to be criticized. In fact, children see their parents' faults all too clearly, and if you can say to a child, 'Yes, your dad drinks far too much, and he's a sod when he's drunk,' then at least the child knows what he feels about his father's behaviour is real, and his disapproval is right. But then you can go on to explain why the father drinks and thereby give the child an objective view of his own family.

People always underestimate the ability of children to understand what is going on in their parents' lives. It is one of my principal jobs to teach mothers and children to accept that they have been damaged by their experiences. I point out that if they had had a severe car crash they would have received expert care and attention in a hospital, and have been an object of everyone's concern. Because we, as a society, have buried our heads in the sand, we do not wish to recognize that the injuries sustained behind the front door, at the hands of a partner who is supposed to love and cherish you, can be so much worse. The bruises and bones can heal, but the internal personal damage will take years to mend. A woman or man who has been mentally tortured by his partner will show far worse damage than that of the occasional furious fistfight. The slow corroding of a personality that occurs with unkind treatment takes a lot of healing. Only warm, loving approval will do that.

That is what Chiswick Women's Aid can do with the mothers and children. If the women are bitter about their men, I remind them that if I had not had my particular childhood, if my father had not ill-treated my mother, there would have never have been a called 'Chiswick Women's Aid'. Therefore my father's life was valuable, as indeed is that of every human being I have ever met.